DESIGN THINKING MENTOR BOOK

Creating "the New" as "a Team"

Table of Contents

ISBN: 978-605-86037-6-9

Preface

This book aims to help you create "the new" as "a team" by applying design thinking and doing. It includes:

- the most effective design thinking tools and techniques that will help business and development teams "think together" with design thinking and "do together" with agile methodology.

- practical tips tested in more than 50 design thinking workshops that will guide you in facilitating your own workshops and creating most desirable products, services, customer experiences (CX), employee experiences (EX) and user experiences (UX).

- inspiring quotes and stories from prominent artists, philosophers, scientists, and business people that will make you a storyteller during the facilitation of design thinking workshops.

- ways of applying design thinking with other human-centered methodologies such as agile, lean startup and UX design.

- artful thinking practices for invoking creativity, empathy, insightful thinking, and other right- brain skills of workshop participants.

- case studies that show the outcomes of "design thinking" and results of "design doing."

- real-life examples of how design thinking can help you to become a more agile, innovative, customer-centric, collaborative, and digitalized organization.

As an extension of Design Thinking Methodology book, we hope this book will guide and inspire you to transform your businesses, technologies and organizations.

About the Author

Emrah Yayici is the author of the bestselling books: *Business Analysis Methodology, Business Analyst's Mentor, UX Design and Usability Mentor, Artful Thinking* and *Design Thinking Methodology.*

He is a managing partner of UXservices, BA-Works, Keytorc, and ArtBizTech. He began his career as a technology and management consultant at Arthur Andersen and Accenture. Afterwards, he led global enterprise-transformation projects at Beko-Grundig Electronics.

During his career, he has managed multinational and cross-functional project teams in banking, insurance, telecommunications, media, consumer electronics, IT industries, and start-ups.

Emrah Yayici contributes to IIBA® (International Institute of Business Analysis) as a chapter president. He is also a member of and contributor to UXPA (User Experience Professionals Association) and, as a former international board member, a contributor to ISTQB® (International Software Testing Board).

He is now sharing his experience in design thinking, business analysis, strategic design, service design, customer experience design, employee experience design and user experience design by publishing articles and books, leading training sessions, and speaking at conferences.

1. How Should You Plan Design Thinking Workshops?

In recent years, start-ups, large enterprises, and nonprofit organizations have increasingly used design thinking to foster innovation and create desirable solutions, products, services, and experiences. In addition to being a mindset, design thinking is a methodology that is applied in workshop format. A typical workshop usually lasts two days. However, there is preliminary work that should be completed before the workshop. Design thinking methodology includes six phases:

1- Definition

A design thinking initiative starts with a meeting to define the challenge and target user groups (personas).

2- Research

Before the workshop, teams often conduct research by interviewing and observing target users in their natural environments. This preliminary research is usually completed within one or two weeks and helps research teams to frame the challenge and begin to empathize with target users.

In order to better understand their needs and expectations, research teams invite users to the workshop. The interview sessions conducted with users are completed during the first half of day one.

3- Interpretation

During the second half of day one, workshop participants analyze the results of research efforts and identify insights that will become the basis for ideation.

4- Idea Generation

During the first half of day two, participants conduct an ideation session. They then prioritize ideas according to their proposed value and difficulty of implementation.

5- Prototyping

During the second half of day two, workshop participants prototype selected ideas and prepare them for evaluation as solution concepts.

6- Evaluation

During the last part of the workshop, users comment on and answer questions pertaining to prototyped solution concepts. This session also creates an opportunity to generate additional insights and solution ideas.

2. Which Techniques Can You Apply at Each Phase of Design Thinking Methodology?

Pablo Picasso once said, "Learn the rules like a pro, so you can break them like an artist." Design thinking is very similar to artistry in the sense that applying techniques is a silver bullet in the creation of the most desirable solutions.

DEFINITION PHASE

- **HMW Questions Technique**

Design thinking teams can use the "how might we" (HMW) questions technique to define and frame the workshop challenge.

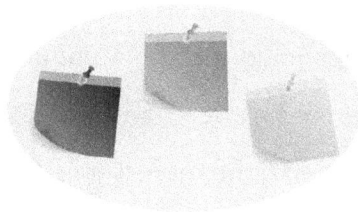

HMW questions should not be too broad or too narrow.

- Ineffective Design Challenge Definitions:

    o "How might we be a more successful company?" (too broad)

    o "How might we improve the sales of our dealers at remote locations by adding a dealer search page on the mobile app?" (too narrow)

- Effective Design Challenge Definition:

o "How might we improve the sales of our dealers at remote locations?" (neither too broad nor too narrow)

- **Persona**

Identifying personas is the best way to define target user groups. Although many different user groups may exist, design thinking teams should limit the number of personas to three (at most four, in extreme cases) in order to prevent falling into the trap of "designing for everybody."

A persona description should include a name, photo, and demographic info (such as age, gender, education, and profession), as well as a scenario section that best represents the mental model of the persona.

One of the main principles of design thinking is human-centricity. Emotional design is one important aspect of human centricity. Human beings judge things based on the left-brain's logical and right-brain's emotional capabilities, but most of the time, emotion is the main criterion in their judgments.

In alignment with their emotions, users first create a mental model of the products they use. This model guides them throughout their experience with the product. Therefore, solutions should be based on the mental models of users rather than those of designers.

This can be accomplished by including the interests, capabilities, weaknesses, and expectations of the persona in the persona description. These psychological aspects of the persona can be defined in the scenario section of the persona description.

RESEARCH & INTERPRETATION PHASES

- **Interviews**

The aim of interviews is to collect as much research data as possible about the needs and expectations of target users by asking them specific and unbiased questions during preliminary research and the workshop.

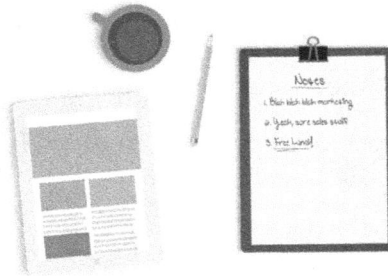

To increase the effectiveness of interviews, the following best practices should be applied:

- Don't be afraid to ask questions when something is not clear.

- Avoid making assumptions. Question the rationale behind interviewees' statements.

- Listen more and talk less.

- Prepare simple, objective, and to-the-point questions before interviews. Don't ask biased questions.

- Be open-minded and prevent shallow "either/or" discussions.

- **Contextual Analysis**

Preliminary to the workshop, design thinking teams should observe users in their own environments (context) to pinpoint user needs and problems that might not be identified during interviews. "Context" is often confused with "content," but they are completely different concepts. The definition of context in business, art, and other fields is very similar to its meaning in archaeology. For an archaeologist, context means the place where an artifact is found. The artifact itself (content) does not provide enough information to make predictions about history; it should be evaluated together with the attributes of the place where it is found. Similarly, analyzing an artwork requires consideration of contextual factors—such as social, political, and ecological conditions—of the time during which it was created. Impressionist artists, for instance, were interested in context as much as in content. The most famous impressionist painters — Eduard Manet, Claude Monet, Edgar Degas, Camille Pissarro, Alfred Sisley, and Pierre-August Renoir — predominantly painted landscapes and scenes from life, capturing the momentary effect of light by painting *en plein air*, or in the open air. In order to best perceive and present contextual factors in their paintings, Impressionist artists took leave of the studio to paint in nature. Monet's *Impression, Sunrise* gave the Impressionism movement its name. Monet painted the same subject on multiple canvases at different times of the day. In this manner, he depicted different perspectives of the same content as the context changed due to the changing light. At the time, Impressionist paintings were highly criticized because they challenged traditional standards of painting; now, they are recognized as the first modern movement in art.As in archeology and art, design thinking teams should take context into account because it is one of the most important factors affecting human behavior in their use of products, technologies, services, or spaces. This can easily be observed at banks, where there are many alternative contact points with customers. Due to contextual factors, user behavior is different at each channel. For example, while live video chat technology is an effective customer service solution for internet banking users, it may not be appropriate for ATM users, as customers waiting in the queue would become impatient.

- **Customer Journey Map**

Journey mapping is an effective technique used to visualize and evaluate the end-to-end experience of users during their engagement with a product or service at different touch points. It provides a holistic representation of each persona group's needs, expectations, emotions, motivations, and satisfaction level at each stage of their experience.

For instance, the customer activities in various channels of a utility services company as they search for service details, apply for subscriptions on the web page, complete subscriptions at a dealer by signing a contract, receive an invoice via e-mail, and make inquiries via the call center can be visualized and evaluated by using the journey mapping technique. In this way, design thinking teams can gain insights into improving customer experience in each existing interaction channel.

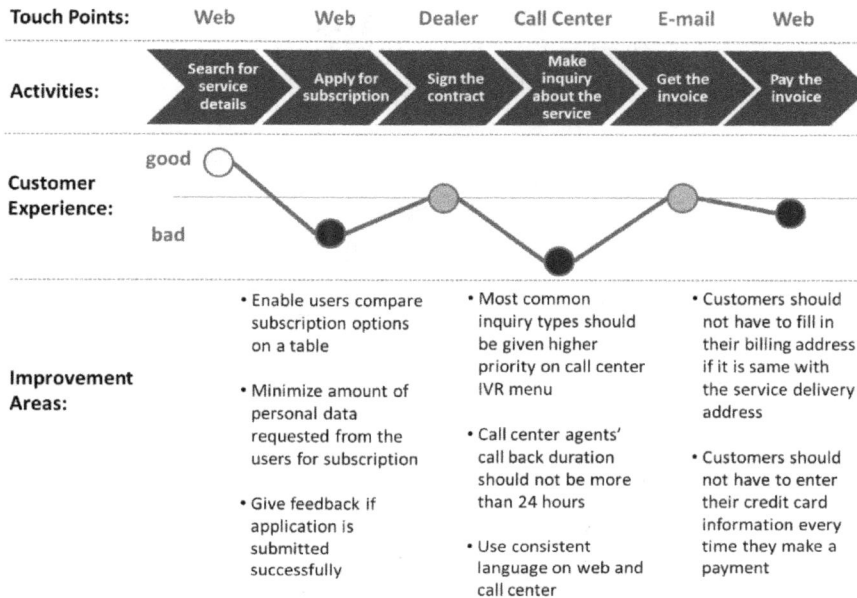

Touch Points:	Web	Web	Dealer	Call Center	E-mail	Web
Activities:	Search for service details	Apply for subscription	Sign the contract	Make inquiry about the service	Get the invoice	Pay the invoice

Customer Experience: good / bad

Improvement Areas:

- Enable users compare subscription options on a table
- Minimize amount of personal data requested from the users for subscription
- Give feedback if application is submitted successfully

- Most common inquiry types should be given higher priority on call center IVR menu
- Call center agents' call back duration should not be more than 24 hours
- Use consistent language on web and call center

- Customers should not have to fill in their billing address if it is same with the service delivery address
- Customers should not have to enter their credit card information every time they make a payment

- **Empathy Mapping**

Design thinking is an empathy-driven methodology which promotes emotional design. It requires treating people not as subscribers, but as human beings who form emotional bonds to the products, services, or spaces they use. In other words, it positions people as "subjects" rather than "objects." In generating insights, therefore, design thinking teams should consider not only the needs and problems of target users, but also their emotions. They can apply the empathy mapping technique to uncover, visualize, and better understand the target user's emotional experience in the given situation by synthesizing research data. It is a very effective tool to generate insights that are not obvious.

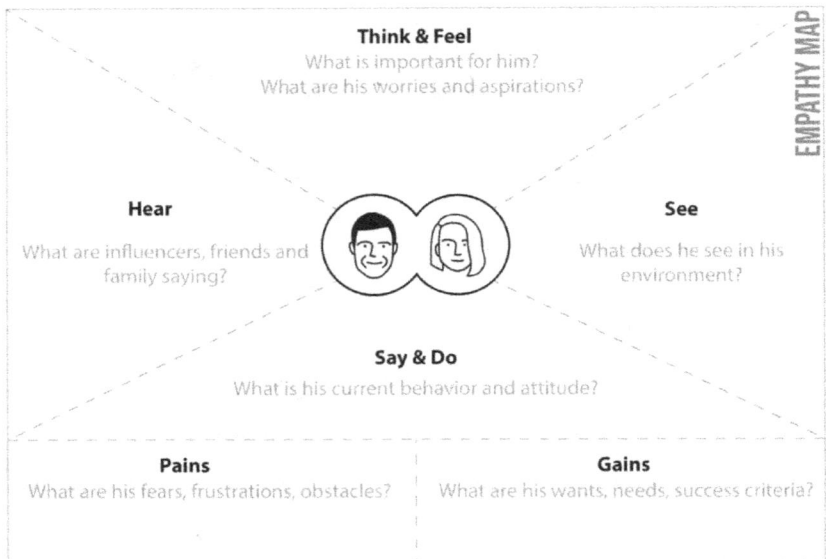

EMPATHY MAP

Think & Feel
What is important for him?
What are his worries and aspirations?

Hear
What are influencers, friends and family saying?

See
What does he see in his environment?

Say & Do
What is his current behavior and attitude?

Pains
What are his fears, frustrations, obstacles?

Gains
What are his wants, needs, success criteria?

Empathy maps should be prepared for each persona group by applying the following steps:

- Hang an empathy mapping sheet on the whiteboard for each selected persona.

- Analyze research results about the persona group and discuss their feelings about the current situation. Note the impressions of their influencers.

- Watch video recordings of the preliminary research phase.

- Fill in each section of the empathy mapping sheet.

- Repeat these steps for each persona group.

- Finally, analyze all of the notes on the empathy maps and generate actionable insights from the most prominent emotional patterns.

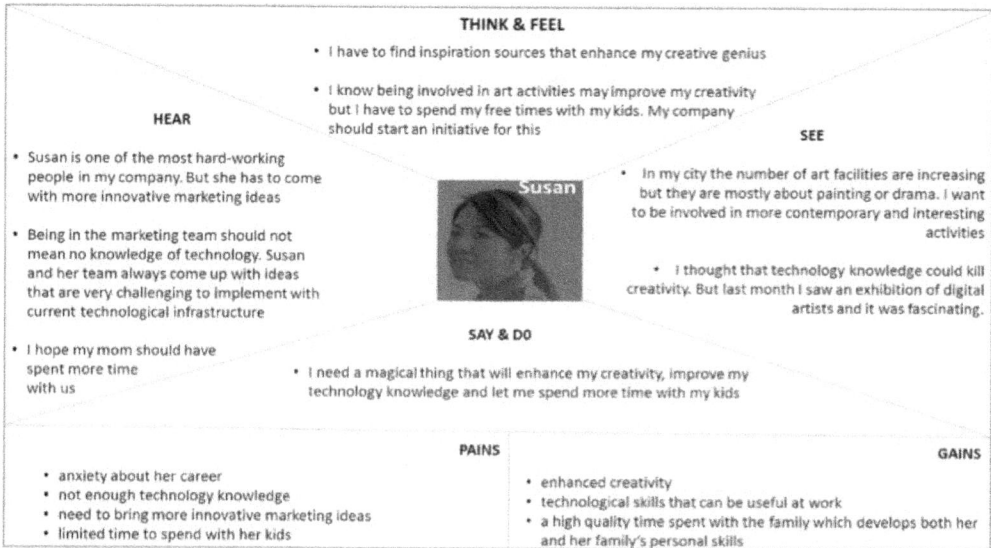

- Mind-Mapping

Mind-mapping is an effective technique used to break down complex problems into smaller parts and then analyze the root causes behind them in order to drive actionable insights. It is similar to famous philosopher Jacques Derrida's approach of deconstructing texts and reinterpreting them to explore new meanings.

Insights are usually driven by attempting to uncover the root causes of user problems identified during the research phase. Design thinking teams may sometimes feel desperate when they confront tough problems. Rather than giving up, they should remain optimistic and remember the advice of Henry Ford, who said, "There are no big problems; there are just a lot of little problems."

Design thinking teams can apply this functional decomposition approach via mind-mapping by dividing problems into smaller parts and then analyzing the root causes behind them. As strategy guru Peter Drucker said, "The most important thing in communication is to hear what isn't being said." Mind-mapping makes the invisible visible by uncovering the root causes of problems.

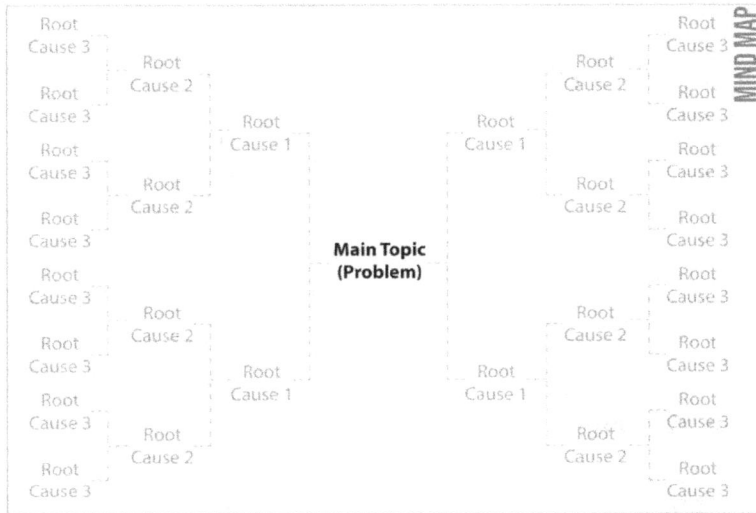

The mind mapping technique can be applied as follows:

- Set up a whiteboard, markers, and sticky notes.

- Write the problem as a keyword at the center of the map.

- Position it as the main topic (problem).

- Separate the main topic into simpler, first-level subtopics (root causes of the problem).

- Use simple visual elements to represent each first-level subtopic.

- Use branches to connect first-level subtopics to the main topic.

- Continue to divide these topics into second, third, and nth-level subtopics based on more detailed cause and effect relationships.

- After completing the tree diagram, generate insights by analyzing subtopics and the relationships between them.

- **Affinity Diagram**

The affinity diagram is a popular technique used to group large amounts of research results under specific categories and then generate insights by analyzing the connections between these groupings.

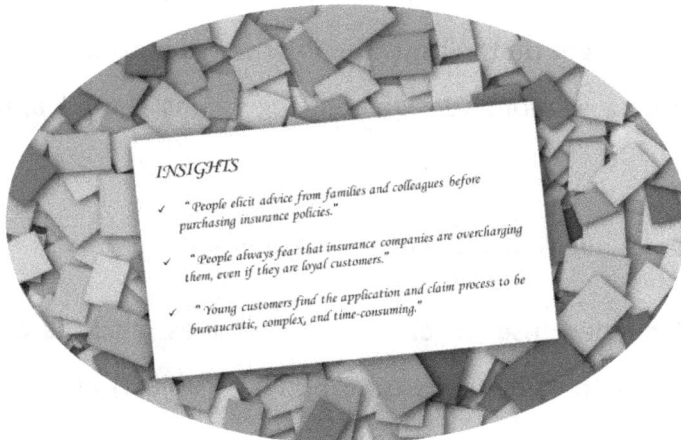

The affinity diagram technique is applied as follows:

- First, write each research finding on a separate sticky note and place them on a whiteboard.

- Group sticky notes together, based on common characteristics.

- Assign a category name to each group.

- Begin to identify the relationships between each category and, if possible, reorganize them under superheaders.

- Analyze the affinity diagram and, based on similarities, dependencies and repetitions, explore patterns among the research data.

- Finally, use the above patterns to generate actionable insights.

IDEATION PHASE

- **Brainstorming**

Brainstorming is the spontaneous listing of creative ideas, without placing too much thought on their quality. In order to maximize the effectiveness of brainstorming sessions, design thinking teams should apply the following best practices:

- Invite all of the relevant stakeholders.

- If needed, use ice-breaking techniques (such as asking participants about their opinions on a popular subject) at the beginning of the session to inspire collaboration.

- At the beginning of the meeting, review the design challenge, research results, and insights uncovered during the previous phases.

- When needed, steer participants to generate solution ideas related to the design challenge.

- In order to provide encouragement, do not judge the quality of the participants' ideas.

- In order to encourage those who best express their ideas by drawing, make whiteboards available.

- Motivate participants to think creatively, and ask them to generate as many ideas as possible. Remind them that their ideas do not have to be realistic or achievable.

- Do not evaluate the feasibility of solution ideas during brainstorming sessions. Such details should be discussed during prioritization sessions at the end of the ideation phase.

- **Brain Dump**

If participants are hesitant to share their ideas in front of others, design thinking teams can apply the brain dump technique.

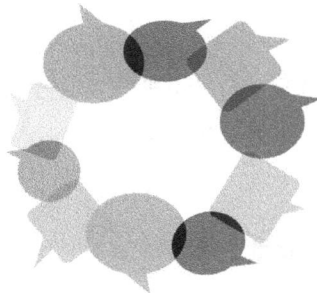

This technique is applied as follows:

- Instead of verbally sharing ideas, participants write them down on sticky notes by discussing with other people in their group.

- The facilitator reminds each group to complete this process within the time allocated.

- When the time is up, each group presents their ideas to the entire team.

- **Reverse Brainstorming**

If participants have difficulty in generating creative ideas, design thinking teams can apply the reverse brainstorming technique. This technique approaches problems in reverse. For example, if the objective is improving customer experience at the call center, then the team questions how customers can have a worse experience. They brainstorm how they can cause the problem instead of how they can solve it. Then they use these root causes as a basis to generate solutions for the original problem.

- **Benchmarking Technique**

Design thinking teams should focus not only on creating functional and usable solutions, but also on desirable solutions that have an aura. Whether it is a product, service, or experience, desirability is the "gotta have it impact" of an object. Originality determines the aura, as well as an object's "gotta have it" impact. The most original solutions are those that satisfy people's needs in the most creative ways. Thus, design thinking teams should focus on creating original solutions instead of reproducing those of its competitors. Before discussing competitor solutions, they should first focus on generating original solution ideas during the ideation phase. Therefore, benchmarking studies should be presented to workshop participants after ideation is over.

- **Prioritization**

At the end of the ideation session, design thinking teams should apply convergent thinking and prioritize solution ideas according to two main criteria:

- value proposition, and

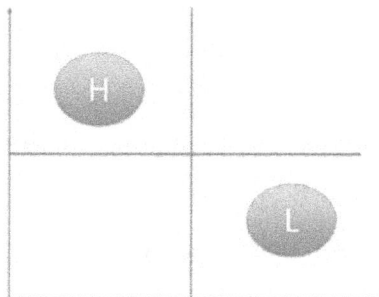

- difficulty of implementation.

During prioritization, a solution idea can be disregarded if it's difficult to implement, even if it is of high value proposition.

Difficulty of implementation is usually a matter of financial and technical limitations. Current advances in technology allow us to realize most kinds of creative ideas. However, such technologies can be costly, making financial considerations an important part of the evaluation of alternative solution ideas.

During prioritization sessions, ideas with high value propositions and low implementation difficulty should be rated as high priority, whereas those with low value propositions and high implementation difficulty should be rated as low priority. Design thinking teams should first prototype and evaluate high priority ideas before assessing the implementation of low priority ideas. As Coco Chanel said, "Luxury is a necessity that begins where necessity ends."

Value Proposition

Implementation Difficulty

Even in time-sensitive, fast-track projects, some perfectionist stakeholders might insist on expanding the solution scope with low priority ideas. But as Voltaire writes in his poem "La Bégueule," "Perfect is the enemy of good." In other words, insisting on perfection often results in no improvement at all.

Even artists cannot always achieve perfection, despite their meticulous characters. Throughout history, artists have struggled to create masterpieces with the highest level of detail. The most prominent example of this is the use of the golden ratio — also known as the divine proportion — which is applied to achieve balance and beauty in sculptures and paintings. The golden ratio of an object is found when the longer part divided by the smaller part is also equal to the whole length divided by the longer part. Leonardo da Vinci applied the golden ratio to define all proportions in *The Last Supper*, *Vitruvian Man*, and the *Mona Lisa*.

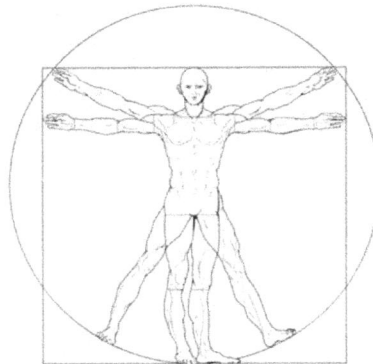

Other artists such as Michelangelo, Raphael, Rembrandt, Georges Seurat, and Salvador Dali also applied the golden ratio to reach the highest level of aesthetic perfection. For example, the ratio of the dimensions of Dali's painting *The Sacrament of the Last Supper* adheres to the golden ratio. Due to his high self-esteem and passion for perfection, Dali had trouble in his early career. He was even expelled from school after criticizing his teachers for not having enough talent to be able to comment on the perfection of his artworks. But later in his career, even he accepted the idea that perfection has no limits. He summarized this belief as follows: "Have no fear of perfection—you'll never reach it." Similarly, Johann Wolfgang von Goethe once said, "In art the best is good enough."

- Value Proposition Canvas Technique

During prioritization, design thinking teams can use the value proposition canvas technique to assess the value of solution ideas in terms of satisfying the needs and wants of target users. The value proposition canvas is a complementary technique to the empathy map. It shows how target users can benefit from new solution ideas in achieving expected gains and relieving the pains listed on empathy maps.

PROTOTYPING & EVALUATION PHASE

- Low Fidelity Prototyping

Many teams can generate creative ideas, but they may not be able to turn them into tangible solutions. Prototyping allows design thinking teams to visualize and turn imaginary solution ideas into tangible forms which help them communicate with users to gain a better understanding of how an idea might solve the addressed challenge. Prototypes are the medium where the abstract and concrete first meet. In addition to the concretization of ideas, prototypes are also helpful in gathering early user feedback. Making iterations on the final solution is costly because for every iteration, the solution's components must be changed and retested, whereas changing the prototype is much easier and faster. By prototyping, design thinking teams can adapt, learn from failures in initial iterations, and apply previous experiences to later ones. Prototyping requires only simple materials such as cardboard, sticky notes, paper, and pencils. Graphic design tools are sometimes used for prototyping, although they are not necessary. In fact, using such tools may mislead the team, shifting the focus from conceptual design to visual details such as color and font types. Creating more detailed prototypes is a part of UX design rather than design thinking workshops.

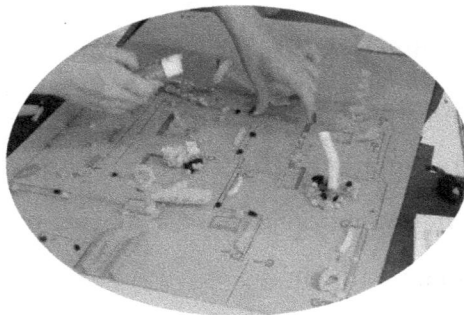

During prototyping and evaluation sessions, the simplicity of the proposed solution should also be assessed. The best solutions are simplistic and intuitive ones. Complex solutions can make an experience difficult for users. As psychologist Barry Schwartz says in his book *The Paradox of Choice: Why More Is Less*, choice overload can result in decision-making paralysis, anxiety, and stress. People fail to complete tasks when their cognitive loads reach a certain limit.

- **Storyboards**

If the solution to design challenge is not new software, product, or space but an intangible solution such as a new service, business model, or process, then design thinking teams can use the storyboard technique to prototype and evaluate solutions.

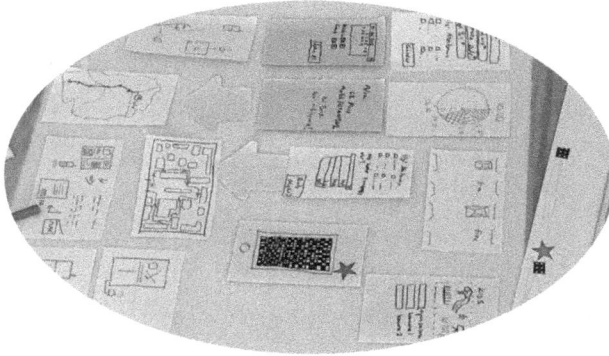

As in filmmaking, the new solution may be presented by visualizing user interactions as a story that is graphically represented with images in sequential sections and frames. This does not require advanced drawing skills and can easily be created with a pen and paper. The pictures do not have to be perfect, but they should be easily understandable.

- **Role Playing**

Role playing is another technique used to prototype intangible solutions such as new services and processes. Workshop participants are assigned roles pertaining to the new solution concept and then play out those roles while evaluations are made.

Storyboarding prior to role playing makes the new solution concept clearer and maximizes the effectiveness of evaluation sessions.

3. How Can You Turn Design Thinking Into Design Doing?

As Sarah Ban Breathnach said, "The world needs dreamers and the world needs doers. But above all, the world needs dreamers who do."

Thinking without Doing

Innovative companies turn imagination into creativity by being not only design thinkers but also design doers. Companies can fully benefit from the solution ideas generated at design thinking workshops when they realize them as new products, services, and experiences. Without doing so, the return of investment of design thinking efforts remains very low.

Doing without Thinking

Doing without thinking leads to worse results. For instance, traditional project lifecycles that do not incorporate design thinking adhere to the following approach:

- business units identify a problem or an opportunity,

- they predict the best solution option and send their request to development teams through demand management systems,

- a BA (business analysis) team meets with business unit representatives several times to determine the solution scope and detailed requirements, and

- after development and testing processes, the solution is sent for UAT (user acceptance test). This is the first and last time that end users are involved in the project throughout the entire project lifecycle.

The success rate of this classical approach in which solutions are created *for* users but not *with* them is very low. Despite the hard work of business analysts and development teams, only a small percentage of these projects are completed within target project timelines and budgets. And most of the time, the project ends with a solution in which target users have no interest. Businesses blame development teams for delivering a solution that does not meet their expectations. They also frequently claim that due to late delivery of the proposed solution, it has lost its importance in rapidly changing market conditions and fierce time-to-market pressures. On the other side, development teams criticize business units for never-ending CRs (change requests) during the project. Project latencies and unpredictable project costs are associated with these CRs. Development teams claim that the business did not know what it really needed. The drawbacks of this classical project lifecycle can be summarized as follows:

- Unclear project goals and scope

   Business and development teams do not have a common and clear understanding of project goals, project scope, and target users. As Amazon CEO Jeff Bezos said, "Unrealistic beliefs on scope—often hidden and undiscussed—kill high standards."

- No user involvement

   End users are not involved in analysis, design, and development stages. Businesses are confident that they know users' needs better than the users, themselves, do. The solution scope and requirements are defined based on assumptions rather than real user needs and insights.

- Limited Collaboration

   Business and development teams work in a silo-based structure. Rather than working in a collaborative team, they progress with formal sign-offs to avoid responsibility for potential project failure.

Thinking + Doing Together

To prevent this "doing without thinking" situation, high-performing companies integrate design thinking into demand management, scope definition, project management, requirements analysis, design, development, release, and test processes. In these companies, business and development teams "think together" and "do together" by applying the following steps:

- When a business unit identifies a business problem, the root causes of the problem are first analyzed.

  There are usually three types of business problems:

  1. Known / Knowns: The root cause of the business problem is definitely known.

  2. Known / Unknowns: Possible root causes of the problem are known.

  3. Unknown / Unknowns: The root cause of the business problem is definitely unknown.

Design thinking is especially effective for complex projects with many unknowns. Solving type 2 (complicated) and type 3 (complex) challenges requires a new way of thinking which incorporates aspects of empathy, insightful thinking, and experimentation. Embodying all of these characteristics, design thinking is very effective in solving complex challenges.

- Instead of predicting the best solution option and immediately sending a project request to development teams, the business unit proposes to organize a design thinking workshop. Business unit representatives and business analysts frame the business problem as a challenge statement by using the "how might we" (HMW) questions technique. For instance, if they anticipate benefiting from sales and marketing digitalization but have concerns about dealers' reactions, they might organize a design thinking workshop centered around the following question: "How might we benefit from digital channels while avoiding conflicts with our traditional dealers?" The workshop is designed in lieu of posting a mobile app or web project request on the demand management system.

- After defining the challenge, development teams, business analysts, and business unit representatives from diverse departments are invited to the design thinking workshop. Solutions are collaboratively formulated by leveraging different perspectives within the organization.

- End users representing each persona group are also invited to the design thinking workshop. User-centric techniques such as customer journey and empathy maps are used to identify their needs, expectations, and pain points.

- Additionally, techniques such as affinity diagrams and mind maps are used to identify users' invisible needs and expectations in terms of customer insights. Business analysts then use each outcome as an input to determine the detailed requirements of latter phases of the project.

- Workshop participants focus on generating as many creative ideas as possible and then prioritize them according to their expected value proposition and implementation difficulty. Creating and evaluating all of the ideas collaboratively helps business teams to communicate their priorities more clearly and helps development teams to effectively communicate their constraints.

- The selected ideas are then turned into a solution concept in the form of high level prototypes. End user are again invited to the workshop to evaluate whether this solution concept satisfies their needs and expectations. The solution concept is then revised according to user feedback. A good solution is not only desirable and feasible, but also viable for the business. After using prototypes to collect feedback on the desirability of the solution concept from target users, design thinking teams use business model canvas or lean canvas techniques to evaluate the viability of the proposed solution in terms of different business aspects such as partners, customer segments, costs, and benefits. This canvas-based evaluation results in valuable input in preparation of business case, vision, and scope documents.

- After the workshop, facilitators prepare a design thinking workshop report. The report includes: the challenge statement, personas, user needs and expectations, insights, a list of prioritized ideas, prototype of the solution concept, target user feedback, and an executive summary.

INSIGHTS & IDEAS   PROTOTYPED SOLUTION CONCEPT   SCOPE DOCUMENT

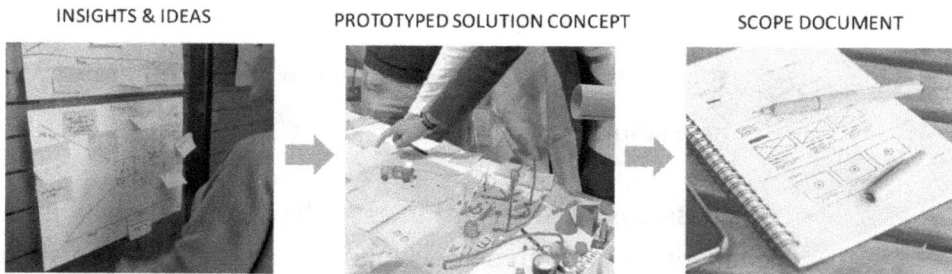

- Business units and business analysts then use the information from the workshop report and the prototype representing the solution concept as inputs to determine solution scope. A typical scope document is defined in the following format:

   o **SOW (Statement of Work) Document:** in case the new solution is a quick win that can be implemented as an enhancement/modification to existing solutions (usually called Type-C projects).

      − A one-page document including a clear definition of the proposed solution describes the scope of the work.

   o **Vision and Scope Document:** in case the solution can be implemented with a medium- or small-scale project (usually called Type-B projects). This document includes:

      − Business requirements: to clarify why the new solution is needed in terms of business perspectives.

      − Scope: to define the user requirements that the solution satisfies. These user requirements (features) mainly correspond to the selected ideas that form the solution conceptualized at design thinking workshops.

- High level architecture: to analyze the relationship of other solutions and systems that will work in integration with the new solution.

o **Business-Case Document:** in case the solution has an enterprise-level impact and can be developed as a large-scale project (usually called Type-A projects). This document is an extended version of the vision and scope document which also includes:

- Cost vs. benefit analysis: to better understand the feasibility of the new solution.

- Risks: to identify and mitigate possible risks of releasing the new solution.

- After all stakeholders have committed to the solution scope, the teams decide on development methodology and release strategy. The two most commonly applied development methodologies are waterfall and agile.

In waterfall projects, development waits for the completion of the analysis and design phases. This latency in delivery can create anxiety for business units who are impatient to see "quick" results. Agile teams, on the other hand, release a working part of the product in a series of two to three weeklong "sprints," without excessive documentation. Agile projects' fast delivery of working products, beginning from the first iteration, instills confidence in all stakeholders and enables the gathering of early customer feedback. In dynamic business environments in which change is not the exception but the norm, applying agile methodology is more meaningful because the waterfall methodology allows for less flexibility in requirements changes. However, applying agile methodology to all projects may not be appropriate. The waterfall methodology, for example, is more appropriate when the solution requires intensive integration among its components, when it is not possible for team members to work on a single project at a time, and when there is high employee turnover, which often results in losing project knowhow.

Project managers should not fall into an either/or fallacy by feeling they have to select either waterfall or agile methodologies. For some projects including both static and dynamic conditions, a hybrid strategy incorporating both waterfall and agile methodologies for different phases within the same project can be applied. Waterfall methodology can be applied at the initial phase of the project to release high-priority, core user requirements of a solution (MVP – minimum viable product) that has a complex architecture of many integrated components, and agile methodology can be applied in later phases to release remaining medium- and low-priority user requirements.

Since the ideas that are generated and prioritized at design thinking workshops form the basis of the solution scope, they play an important role in the selection of development methodology and formulation of the release strategy.

- After deciding on the scope and its release strategy, business analysts elicit detailed functional and non-functional requirements, as well as business rules corresponding to each user requirement in the solution scope.

- Functional requirements: functionalities the solution should have in order to meet user requirements

- Nonfunctional requirements: how the solution should work in terms of quality attributes such as usability, performance, privacy, and security

- Business rules: the conditions, constraints, and formulas that determine how requirements will be handled by the user and the solution

Because they are generated by listening to and observing real users, the user needs and insights identified during design thinking workshops become an important input in the definition of detailed requirements. In waterfall methodology, detailed requirements and business rules are defined in use case documents.

Use Case ID	01
Use Case Name	View and Order a Product
Actors	Customer
Description	Customer searches, finds, orders, and pays for an item.
Preconditions	Customer logs in to the system using an e-mail address and password.
Postconditions	Order confirmation report is sent to the user via e-mail. The dealer delivers the product.

Main Scenario	1. Customer navigates to product selection page.
	2. Customer selects the product category (TV, DVD, speakers, etc.).
	3. Customer views the displayed items under that category and selects a particular one.
	4. Customer views details of the selected item (image, technical specs, color, size, availability, and price).
	5. Customer adds the selected product to the shopping list.
	6. Customer checks the accuracy of items on the shopping list.
	7. Customer checks the total amount of the shopping list on the checkout page.
	8. Customer enters shipping address.
	9. Customer enters billing address.
	10. Customer enters credit or debit card information.
	11. Customer confirms the payment.
	12. Customer views Order Confirmation Report.
	13. Dealer gets the order (BR2).
	14. Dealer delivers the product to the customer.
Alternative Scenario	1.1. Customer does a search for the product instead of navigating through the relevant category.
	1.2. Customer views search results and selects the item he or she is looking for.
	1.3. Back to step 4 of Main Scenario.
Exception Scenario	8.1. If customer selects fast delivery, he or she is notified with a message indicating that a commission rate will be charged for express deliveries (BR1).
	13.1. If the item is out of stock at every dealer, the customer is notified that "the selected product is currently out of stock" (BR2).

Nonfunctional Requirements	NFR 1. Performance: After the customer confirms the payment, the Order Confirmation Report should be displayed within two seconds.
	NFR 2. Usability: If the billing address is same as the delivery address, the customer does not have to enter the same data twice.
Business Rules	BR1. Express Delivery Commission = 1 percent
	BR2. The dealer nearest to the customer's shipping address delivers the ordered item. If the ordered item is out of stock at this dealer, the order is sent to the second-nearest dealer store.
Assumptions	A1. Product availability data received from the ERP inventory module is up to date and accurate.
	A2. Dealer location data received from dealer management system is up to date.

Unlike waterfall methodology, agile methodology focuses on "working products over comprehensive documentation." Therefore, functional and non-functional requirements and business rules are defined as short and simple user stories (As a "role," I want "goal"):

User Story 5	Acceptance Criteria
As a user, I can cancel my order on the mobile application so that I don't have to contact the call center.	• The customer can query her orders. • On the mobile application, the customer can only cancel the orders that have the status of "open" and "in progress." He or she can't cancel the orders that have the status of "delivered."

- As requirements are gathered and documented, user experience designers, service designers, and customer experience designers apply techniques such as interaction design, service blueprinting, and detailed journey mapping to convert requirements into high fidelity design artifacts. In other words, they design each part of the solution concept that was created and prototyped during design thinking workshops.

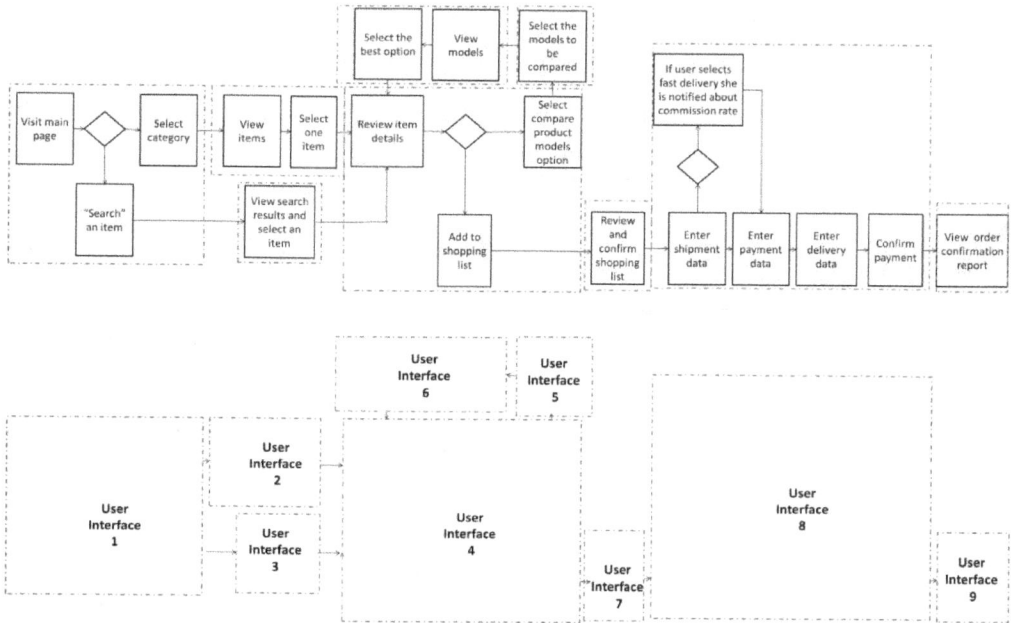

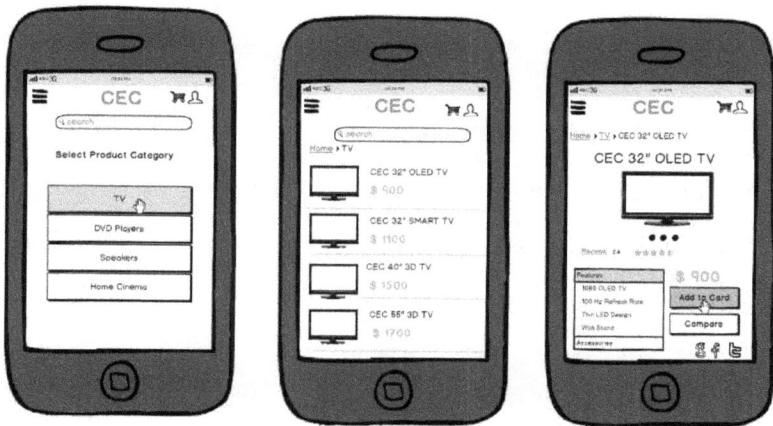

- The usability of design artifacts are then tested by using the prototypes. Project managers sometimes hesitate to allocate specific time and budget for usability testing because they believe that running usability tests requires a fully-equipped test laboratory. While they can be useful, usability labs are not a must-have. In fact, the simple practice of inviting users to the project room to observe their interaction with interfaces can be used to detect and analyze most usability problems. Unlike many other testing types (such as performance), it is possible to test the usability of an incomplete solution by using its prototype. This allows early defect detection and decreases the cost of usability problems.

- Based on requirements and design artifacts, system analysts design the technical architecture of the solution.

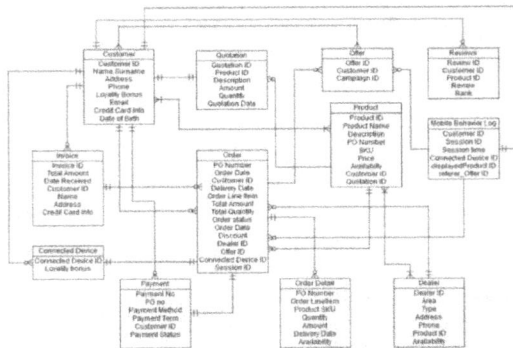

- Finally, development teams use requirement documents and design artifacts to create the products and services. After being tested by quality assurance teams and passing user acceptance tests (UAT), the products and services are then released.

```
....ing sql = getStatement();
resultSet = "select * from st(
if (resultSet = statement.executeQu
result = resultSet.next()) {
setStoreId(resultSet.getInt("s.
storeDescription = res..1
:toreTypeId = r-
:oreAdd-
```

- To mitigate deployment risks such as latencies, high failure rates, and long fixing and recovery times, operations teams apply the DevOps mindset. They participate in design thinking, doing and development efforts in order to be synchronized with other project stakeholders.

Thanks to applying this integrated Design Thinking and Design Doing approach, business and development teams work value-oriented, user-centered, and iterative throughout the project. This helps their company to:

- Be more agile in terms of time to market

- Be more innovative in creating products and services that are driven by real user needs and insights

- Prevent waste by only investing in features that are truly necessary.

4. What are the Lean Principles That Boost the Effectiveness of Design Thinking and Design Doing?

High-performance companies achieve innovation, speed, and quality by injecting the following lean principles into their Design Thinking and Design Doing activities:

Be Value-Oriented

- For each project, focus on generating outcomes (value) rather than outputs (deliverables).

- Always prioritize solution features; focus on "must-haves" rather than "nice-to-haves".

- Eliminate the waste of low-priority features that are not essential for users.

Be Customer-Centered

- Be like the sun but not the moon; illuminate yourself with the light of your customers instead of that of your competitors.

- Rather than benchmarking yourself with your competitors, concentrate on being more responsive to the needs of your target customers.

- Be customer-centric rather than product-centric. Consider products not as an objective but as a tool employed to meet your customers' needs.

- Develop solutions around your customers. Always listen closely to the "voice" of your customers. Set up and maintain a continuous customer feedback loop.

- Ask customers about their needs, not their proposed solutions. As Henry Ford once said, If I had asked people what they wanted, they would have said faster horses."

Be Iterative

- Think big, but start small.

- Be iterative; remember that Rome was not built in a day.

- Move evolutionarily rather than revolutionarily.

- Use prototypes to gather early customer feedback.

- At the initial iteration, release a core version of the solution (MVP – minimum viable product) including only high-priority features.

- In following iterations, use customer feedback from previous releases to refine the solution by adding, updating, and even dropping features.

- Iterate until the solution satisfies business and customer needs.

Be Simplistic

- Remember that less is more. Do not complicate it. Focus on "just enough" — that is, what is really necessary to satisfy customer needs.

- Appreciate downsizing the solution by removing nonessential features rather than upsizing it with bells and whistles.

- Determine solution features as if you are decorating a small house. Don't make users feel claustrophobic by crowding a small space with a lot of furniture.

Don't Be Afraid of Early Failure

- Remember the famous quotation from American scientist and author Dr. James Jay Horning: "Good judgment comes from experience. Experience comes from bad judgment." Be adaptive, learn early from failures in initial iterations, and apply past experiences to future ones.

- Focus on kaizen (continuous improvement) by using lessons learned at previous iterations.

Optimize the Work Flow

- Act "just in time." Analysis and design artifacts represent WIP (work in process) inventories in the development lifecycle. To prevent WIP-level waste, create them at the right moment and with sufficient detail.

5. Do Techniques Kill Creativity?

Some critics contend that using techniques in works that involve design and artistic perspectives kills creativity. But this is not the case, even for the most creative works of art. Throughout history, scientific developments have impacted not only engineering, but also art. English physicist Isaac Newton, for instance, was the first to discover that colors originate from light. He converted white light into red, orange, yellow, green, blue, and violet colors by refracting it off a prism and invented a circular diagram that arranged primary and complementary colors on opposite sides. Artists have since benefited from this diagram to create effective color combinations and contrasts in their paintings. Renaissance artists, in particular, applied advanced techniques in creating their artworks. Some of these techniques include:

- the perspective technique to create the illusion of depth on a two-dimensional canvas based on how the human eye sees the world

  - a linear perspective to show closer objects larger, and more distant objects smaller

- o   a vanishing point to fix the position of artists to their view of the scene by implementing an imaginary horizon and vertical lines

- o   an atmospheric perspective to show that the appearance of objects fades off into the distance

- the foreshortening technique to create the illusion of depth by shortening lines

- the sfumato technique to create three-dimensionality by blurring or softening sharp outlines

- the chiaroscuro technique to create soft, lifelike figures by using a strong contrast between light and dark

- balance and proportion techniques to ensure proper size

With respect to techniques, Leonardo da Vinci is regarded as one of the most accomplished Renaissance artists. He even studied anatomy to develop new universal techniques that he could apply to his art. By applying such techniques, he created incredibly realistic figures in his paintings. The natural style that can be observed in his masterpiece Mona Lisa is a perfect example.

But as everything in life, balance is also important in the usage of standards and techniques. Recognized by its usage of techniques and application of strict rules, Egyptian art is an example of this. Egypt is recognized as one of the most civilized societies in the ancient world, and historians have learned much about this society by analyzing its artwork. To keep their souls alive after death, they created wall paintings for the next life. Egyptian adherence to conservative values led to rigid painting rules for artists. These fixed rules were called the *Canon of Proportion*, or the *Canon*.

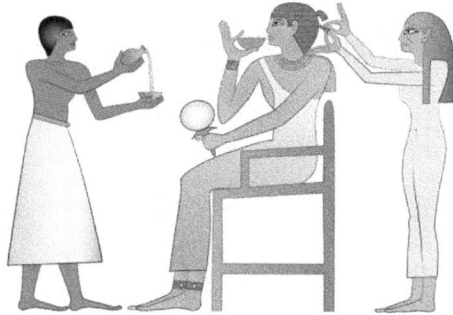

Some of these Canon rules include the following:

- The sizes of figures in paintings were determined by the person's social status instead of by rules of perspective.

- Human figures all looked about the same.

- Parts of the body were shown from different views. The head and feet were shown in profile, and the shoulders and eyes were shown frontally.

- Specific colors were used to express specific emotions. For instance, white represented power and greatness, black represented death, red represented victory and anger, blue represented life, and green represented new life.

These strict standards were applied over the course of hundreds of years. Some historians and sociologists believe that these conservative artistic rules negatively affected the creativity of the society, as well as artistic and scientific progress.

To prevent a similar fate, design thinking teams should not fall into the trap of over-standardization in applying techniques. They should be aware that techniques are like wizards, not magicians. In other words, they have their limits. But they can help teams work more efficiently.

For instance:

- Design thinking teams don't have to limit usage of the HMW (how might we) questions only to defining the challenge; HMW questions can also be used at ideation sessions;

- in addition to the evaluation phase, prototypes can also be used in the research phase to better communicate with target users;

- interviews and user observation techniques can be used in both the research and the evaluation phases; and

- affinity diagrams can be used not only to group and analyze research data, but also to organize ideas generated in ideation sessions.

Design thinking teams should focus on generating outcomes (solutions) rather than outputs (deliverables). The team's objective should not be to produce fancy documents and diagrams. Instead, they should aim to design a solution that best meets the needs of target users. Techniques should be used as tools to make these efforts more convenient.

6. How Many People Should Participate in Design Thinking Workshops?

Three groups of participants participate in design thinking workshops:

- **Facilitators**

The research and prototyping phases of the workshops are very interactive. Therefore, it is not possible to run an effective workshop with only one facilitator. The optimum number of facilitators is two to three people, depending on the number of workshop participants. For effective workshop management and report preparation, facilitators should assign a notetaker for each workshop.

- **Employees from various departments of the company**

Design thinking is best applied by multidisciplinary teams including people with different skills and backgrounds. Therefore, facilitators should invite people from diverse departments of the company. As more people participate in workshops, the power of collective insight and idea generation increases. On the other side, facilitation becomes more difficult. Therefore, the number of workshop participants from different departments of the company should be no less than ten and no more than thirty.

- **End users**

Inviting a limited number of people who represent target personas is much better than inviting many random users to the workshop's research and evaluation phases. The optimum number of users that should be involved in workshops is eight to ten people per persona. In a design thinking workshop with two personas, for example, twenty participants would be more than sufficient. Finding users is one of the most challenging parts of design thinking efforts. In order to find users who represent persona groups, the company's customer database should be carefully analyzed. Before being invited to the workshop, participants should be phone-interviewed, and their social media profiles should be analyzed to ensure that they truly represent their corresponding personas. Design thinking team members' friends and family members may also represent personas and are therefore good candidates for workshop participants, as they can be easily reached and quickly invited to workshops.

7. Should You Invite Company Executives to Design Thinking Workshops?

The participation of executives in design thinking workshops is very valuable due to their experience and vision. Their involvement also increases the likelihood of receiving sponsorship for the implementation of solution ideas generated at the workshops.

Most design thinking teams, however, hesitate to invite company executives. They anticipate that other participants may feel hesitant about sharing their thoughts and ideas in front of them. To mitigate this risk, facilitators should encourage executives to participate as if they were any other member of the team.

At the beginning of the workshop, facilitators should inform every participant that the aim of the workshop is to create "the new" as "a team" and that all thoughts and ideas are welcomed, regardless of existing hierarchies.

8. Where Should You Hold Design Thinking Workshops?

The facilities where design thinking workshops are held affect the energy of participants and performance of facilitators. A location with bright colors, good lighting, air conditioning, and comfortable furniture increases participants' motivation and creative potential.

If possible, organizing design thinking workshops at facilities outside the company location is preferable, as it helps facilitators keep participants focused on the workshop, with minimal interruption by their routine office tasks. Holding workshops in inspiring locations such as near lakes, seasides, or forests (rather than in hotel meeting rooms) will foster participant engagement and creativity.

The workshop location should have enough space to accommodate a roundtable sitting arrangement. It should also have large walls to allow the team to work with sticky notes to communicate needs, insights, and ideas generated during the workshop.

The amount of technological equipment at the workshop location should be kept to a minimum because it may shift the participants' focus from customer-centricity to technology-centricity. The only technological equipment needed to facilitate the workshop is a projector and laptop. To keep participants energetic throughout the workshop, a high-quality sound system to play music during breaks and interactive sessions is also useful.

Facilitators should also ensure that the necessary materials (especially for ideation and prototyping) are available at the workshop's location.

A standard list of design thinking workshop materials are as follows: Flip charts, colored cardboards, A4 paper, post-it notes in different colors and sizes, colored pens, pencils, pencil sharpeners, and erasers, perforated stapler and staples, scissors, glue stick, colored adhesive tape, colored straws, sticker sets (such as emoji, hearts, or colored circles), paper clips, colored foil paper, color felt (A4 size), colored corrugated cardboard (A4 size), colorful wooden sticks.

9. How Can You Integrate Design Thinking, Lean Startup, and Agile Methodologies?

Design thinking should be regarded not as an alternative, but as complementary to lean startup and agile methodologies.

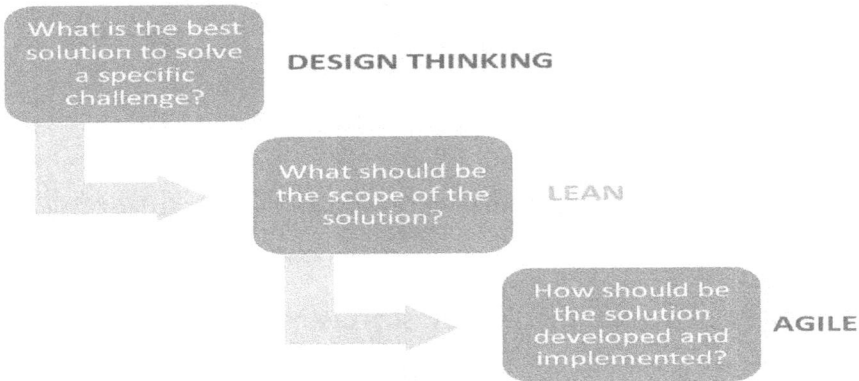

These methodologies can be applied throughout product and service development lifecycles as follows:

1. **First, design thinking methodology should be applied to identify the best solution concept:**

   Doing the right thing is always more important than doing it right. Therefore, organizations should first apply design thinking methodology to identify the right solution concept for their challenge.

   During design thinking workshops, participants identify target users' needs, turn them into actionable insights, and generate ideas based on these insights. Then, all ideas are prioritized according to their value proposition and implementation difficulty. Afterwards, selected ideas are prototyped, and a solution concept is created. The solution concept is finalized according to target user feedback on the prototypes.

2. **Then, the lean startup approach should be applied to define the scope and release strategy of the solution that is conceptualized during design thinking workshops.**

In the lean startup approach, the initial version of the solution is called MVP (minimum viable product). MVP has the minimum set of features that satisfies target users' main needs and expectations. High-priority ideas (WOWs) generated during design thinking workshops are the best candidates for the MVP. Medium- and low-priority ideas can be added to later releases based on user feedback on the core version. The priority of ideas may change based on customer feedback on the released versions. A feature that was initially considered low-priority may later become high-priority. Similarly, a feature that was initially considered high-priority may become obsolete if it doesn't deliver the desired value to users after release.

3. **Finally, agile methodology should be applied to develop and implement the solution conceptualized during design thinking workshops. This should occur in alignment with the release strategy formulated by the lean startup approach.**

One of the manifesto statements of agile methodology is: "Working solutions over comprehensive documentation." In Scrum, a popular agile framework, requirements are defined as short and simple user stories (as a "role," I want "goal") about the product backlog. These stories, usually told by a business unit representative (the product owner), minimize the level of documentation and bureaucracy involved in waterfall projects. The agile team releases the working parts of the solution in a series of two to three week long "sprints." Agile projects' fast delivery of working solutions, beginning with the first iteration, brings confidence to all stakeholders. However, if the agile team does not have visibility on the solution concept, fast delivery can result in chaos and huge refactoring efforts in later sprints. Therefore, the prioritized solution ideas and prototyped solution concept generated at design thinking workshops create foresight for high level product backlog and ensure that all team members are on the same page concerning the scope and conceptual architecture of the solution.

In sum, design thinking is more about answers to "why" and "what" questions, lean startup is primarily about answers to "what" and "when" questions, and agile is more about answers to "how" question in product and service development lifecycles. As it was said at the beginning of the movie *Now You See Me,* "the closer you look, the less you see." From start to end, maintaining a bird's-eye, holistic view of the project can keep product and service development teams focused on the big picture (the challenge). This kind of holistic approach helps development teams ensure an organic unity in answering *Why, What,* and *How* questions throughout the project.

Similarly, the most valued artworks are also a result of organic unity. The practice of understanding the organic unity of an artwork's content, subject, and form can help business and technology teams achieve the organic unity of why, what, and how questions when developing new products and services.

Pablo Picasso's famous painting Guernica is a perfect example of this organic unity.

Why	Content	*"My whole life as an artist has been nothing more than a continuous struggle against reaction and the death of art. In the picture I am painting—which I shall call Guernica—I am expressing my horror of the military caste which is now plundering Spain into an ocean of misery and death."* (Pablo Picasso) *Guernica* makes a powerful political statement about the tragedy of war and the suffering of innocent civilians. It was created in response to the bombing of Guernica, a village in Spain. Since it was painted in 1937, it has become an antiwar symbol. Upon seeing a photo of *Guernica*, an officer asked Picasso, "Did you do that?" Picasso responded, "No, *you* did."
What	Subject	The scene features dead bodies, terrified animals, and a woman who is grieving over the dead child in her arms. It shows that not only human beings but also animals share the horror of war.
How	Form	Broken, hard-edged, geometric shapes reminiscent of the cubist art movement are used. The monochromatic style, with black being the predominant color, brings to mind death and violence.

10. Why Has Design Thinking Become So Important for Agile Companies?

In classical product development methodologies, business analysts work with business units to define scope and detailed requirements. In theory, however, business analysts do not play a role in agile projects. They are replaced by product owners, who are usually selected from business units. The product owner is responsible for defining the requirements in user story format and prioritizing them in a repository called the product backlog. The product backlog also represents the solution scope.

A product owner should have a good level of business knowledge and experience in order to make accurate and complete requirements definitions. In most companies, however, business unit managers prefer to assign junior employees to projects as product owners. They assign experienced employees for critical business activities in their own departments. In addition to experience, junior business representatives also lack requirements elicitation and management skills. This makes scope definition and management extremely risky for agile projects and results in ever-increasing technical debt at each sprint.

To mitigate this risk, an experienced business analyst (rather than employee from the business units) can be assigned to the product owner role. In the case that the product owner is selected from business units, the agile team should also include business analysts, as well as developers and testers.

Another effective way of mitigating this scope (product backlog) risk is to organize design thinking workshops before the kickoff of agile projects. Workshops can help to steer all project stakeholders in the same direction regarding solution scope and project objectives.

- At the initial phase of the workshop, the agile team contributes to the definition of the challenge statement, which then becomes the project's main objective. As part of the workshop team, they are also involved in clarification of target users. At later phases of the project, this helps them remember that the real users that should be satisfied are the end users, not business representatives.

- At the research phase of the design thinking workshop, the team identifies user needs and pain points by listening to "what users say" through interviews and by observing "what users do" through contextual analysis. They then systematically turn this research data into actionable insights. This motivates them to create the baseline for both useful and desirable solutions at each sprint.

- Generating user stories from ideas created during design thinking workshops is a very practical and complementary approach. Each idea is prioritized by assessing its value proposition for the user and its implementation difficulty. Depending on their priority assessment, the ideas are labelled as "wows: high value ideas that can be implemented without too much difficulty," "hows: ideas for the future," and "nows: quick wins". This data is very valuable for agile teams in prioritizing user stories within the product backlog and in sprint planning.

- The ideas are prototyped and turned into a solution concept during design thinking workshops. This solution concept is used both to bring ideas into tangible forms and to receive user feedback. This prototyped solution concept encourages the whole agile team to be on the same page. Everyone has a clear idea of what they will do and why they will do it. There is no big upfront design for agile projects. Therefore, this high level conceptual prototype and workshop report contribute greatly to reducing unknowns at the start of the agile project and in mitigating the technical debt risk due to these unknowns.

11. What Is the Difference Between Design Thinking and UX Design?

Although Design Thinking and UX (user experience) Design share many tools and techniques, they are different concepts. UX design is a broad field of tools, techniques, principles, and guidelines that is used to design useful, usable, and desirable experiences. On the other hand, design thinking is a mindset and toolkit that can be used not only in the design of experiences, services, or products, but also in finding creative solutions for any kind of business, social, and everyday challenge.

Design thinking should be applied at the initial phase of each UX design initiative. Based on the insights and conceptual solution ideas generated at each design thinking workshop, UX designers can then begin in-depth research and turn conceptual solutions into detailed design artifacts. In other words, UX design includes both "Design Thinking" and "Design Doing."

Both design thinking and UX design inherit a human-centered and iterative approach.

- **Human-Centric**

Target users are involved throughout design thinking and UX design efforts.

- o At the research phase of design thinking workshops, user needs are identified through interviews, focus groups, and contextual observations. Users are also invited for the evaluation phase to provide feedback on solution ideas.

- o Similarly, for UX design projects, users are involved in both in-depth user research and usability testing activities.

- **Iterative**

Both design thinking and UX design benefit from prototyping.

- o In design thinking, prototypes are used to gather early user feedback on the innovative solution ideas developed during workshops. Therefore, the fidelity of prototypes is very low when compared to those created in the interaction design phase of UX design projects. Even simple storyboards can be used to conceptualize and evaluate the proposed solution ideas formulated at design thinking workshops.

- o For UX design projects, prototyping is necessary to understand whether the new design satisfies the functional needs of users in the most usable way (form follows function). By using prototypes, the usability of the proposed user experience is tested against generally accepted usability criteria such as simplicity, consistency, error prevention, user control, efficiency of use, visibility, and language. Prototypes are also very effective in understanding whether the new user experience satisfies the users in the most engaging way (form follows emotion).

12. Which Skills Must Design Thinkers Possess?

Famous artist Marcel Duchamp once said, "I don't believe in art. I believe in artists." Similarly, companies that apply design thinking have realized that this methodology unleashes its real potential and mitigates the risk of being only a buzzword when design thinking teams exhibit the following skills:

Convergent and Divergent Thinking

As Nietzsche said: "You must have chaos within you to give birth to a rising star." Similarly, the most effective workshops are the ones where ideas dance. Ideas only dance in environments where there is a controlled level of chaos which motivates divergent thinking. Research shows that creativity is best achieved in environments where there is a perfect balance of order and disorder. Therefore, facilitators should behave as curators who turn imagination into creativity by balancing divergent thinking and convergent thinking throughout design thinking workshops.

Positive Thinking

Michelangelo said that inspiration is a combination of encouragement and intelligence. To foster creative ideas, facilitators should not only be able to use effective techniques, but also to keep participants inspired through encouragement. They should ensure that participants maintain a positive mood throughout the workshop. All team members should be optimistic about creating innovative ideas at the workshop. Facilitators should remind participants that, as Victor Hugo said, "Nothing is stronger than an idea whose time has come." Facilitators should then motivate participants by telling them that now is the time. Facilitators should also ensure collaboration by preventing personal egos from getting in the way and by promoting empathy among participants through effective conflict management. When participants encounter conflict, facilitators might remind them of Nobel Prize winner Nikolaas Tinbergen's observation that "There is no white or black in life; there are different tones of gray." When conflicts arise, facilitators should try to create win-win situations, the first rule of which is to ask, "Why does the conflict exist?" The second rule of a win-win situation is to collaboratively find an answer to this question by ignoring personal egos, by behaving objectively, and by being empathic.

Since design thinking workshop participants are grouped as teams sitting at round tables, they may compete with one another to come up with the best ideas. This may create conflict, especially during evaluation and prioritization phases. In this situation, facilitators should strike a balance. Unless competition negatively affects the positive atmosphere in the room, it can act as dopamine for new ideas. History has witnessed the effect of competition in creating "the new" between businesspeople like Steve Jobs and Bill Gates, artists such as Michelangelo and Da Vinci, Picasso and Matisse, and even between two young brothers who created Adidas and Puma after a competition to make the best shoes in their house. If the level of competition begins to spin out of control and/or creates a negative vibe in the room, facilitators should manage the situation by reminding participants that all ideas are owned by the entire organization and that no one will know who thought of that specific idea after the workshop.

Storytelling

When communicating with workshop participants, facilitators should be able to express even the most complex ideas in the simplest forms. Storytelling skills can be very helpful in achieving this, as they can be used to conceptualize and express abstract/complex ideas and emotions. Storytelling is an effective way of communicating a message in a minimal number of words and of using analogies and quotes to persuade and inspire. Friedrich Nietzsche, one of history's most inspiring philosophers and storytellers, once said that his desire was to tell in only ten sentences what others have told in a book.

To improve storytelling skills, facilitators should take note of interesting stories and analogies that they have either heard or experienced in their daily and/or business lives. In other words, they should be collectors of valuable information. In time, they will unexpectedly remember interesting quotes or stories as they discuss a subject. This will help them leave a lasting impression on their audiences.

Hard Work

Without hard work, complete dedication, and full concentration, even the most creative design thinking teams will not be able to create innovative solutions. This is evidenced by the lives of the most creative people—artists. Pablo Picasso, for example, was one of the most hard-working artists of all time. He was always busy producing paintings, sculptures, and ceramics. It is claimed that during the more than seventy-five years of his career, he produced more than ten thousand paintings. Renaissance artists are also extreme examples of the effects of hard work, passion, and dedication.

Michelangelo, for instance, painted *The Creation of Adam* fresco as part of the Sistine Chapel's ceiling in four years, under extremely uncomfortable conditions. For most of the duration, he worked either lying on his back or with his head tilted upward. Leonardo da Vinci, too, spent years analyzing the anatomy of cadavers in order to create masterpieces such as the *Mona Lisa*. Before becoming famous, English rock group The Beatles performed eight hours every day, seven days of the week.

Conceptualization

The information age is being replaced by the conceptual age. In this new age, those who can effectively compose excessive amounts of information as tangible concepts succeed. Therefore, design thinking teams should possess conceptualization skills, since this methodology is mainly about designing a solution through the conceptualization of creative ideas. Teams can improve their conceptualization skills by analyzing how ideas are conceptualized in different forms of artworks. Marcel Duchamp initiated conceptual art by claiming that the most important aspects of an artwork are not the aesthetic details but rather the idea behind its conceptualization . His piece titled *Fountain*, originally a porcelain urinal, is the best example of this. This new way of thinking played an important role in the emergence of today's more abstract and conceptual contemporary art world.

Another way to enhance conceptualization skills is to read philosophy, the art of creating concepts. In his book *Ethica*, for instance, Spinoza created many concepts by using mathematical assertions to propose solutions for a freer and happier life. Similarly, more contemporary philosophers like Deleuze and Foucault created many concepts to help people better understand postmodernism. Reading philosophy is a workout for the brain, a kind of mental gym where our brains' structuring and conceptualization muscles are built.

Thinking Out of the Box

In order to generate creative ideas during workshops, design thinking teams should aim to think out of the box and question the obvious.

As Albert Einstein said, "The problems that exist in the world now cannot be solved by the level of thinking that created them." Archimedes, for instance, calculated the volume and density of objects by placing them in the bathtub and measuring the changing water levels. The object displaced an amount of water equal to its own volume, and the object's density could be calculated by dividing the object's mass by the volume of water it displaced in the bathtub.

Similarly, ultrasonography technology, which enables us to visualize subcutaneous body structures by using sound waves, was discovered by thinking out of the box. Although sound waves are normally used in aural technology, they have also been used in ophthalmic technology. Like radar, this technology was inspired by bats. A bat emits sound waves and listens to the echoes returning back to it to determine how far away an object is, where it is, how big it is, and where it is moving.

Thinking out of the box requires the ability to:

- make paradigm shifts,

- prevent shallow either / or situations, and

- approach problems from different viewpoints.

These skills are best observed in artists. As Oscar Wilde said, "No great artist ever sees things as they really are. If he did, he would cease to be an artist." By thinking out of the box and applying new artistic perspectives, Pablo Picasso created some of the most influential artworks of the twentieth century. His techniques are most evident in his cubist masterpieces. Cubism arose as an alternative art movement more abstract in form than the conventional painting methods that had been applied since the Renaissance. It was a new and revolutionary way of representing the world through painting. Cubism was the result of efforts to paint three-dimensional objects on a two-dimensional canvas. Cubists questioned the classical norm of painting objects from a single perspective. Instead of focusing on a fixed viewpoint, they began to paint different views of an object from different angles, depending on the observer's vision and movement. In this way, they could depict many different elements of an object at once. Picasso's famous painting *The Weeping Woman* is a prime example of this style.

Critical Thinking

Design thinking inherits an evolutionary and experimental approach rather than a revolutionary one. It promotes taking calculated risks by being prepared to fail early and cheaply.

In the evaluation phase, design thinking teams test their prototyped solution with users. They then update the solution in an iterative manner until the solution satisfies user needs and overcomes the challenge defined in the initial phase.

Because critique is a natural part of any effort, including design and artistic efforts, design thinking team members should always appreciate users' critiques of solutions. History has shown that constructive critique often leads to the emergence of new art movements. For instance, it is believed that:

- impressionism evolved from critiques of Monet's paintings,

- cubism evolved from the observation that those paintings were just combinations of cubes, and

- fauvism was born when critic Louis Vauxcelles referred to a group of painters as "fauves" (wild beasts) due to the color tones they used.

These artists did not give up because of critique; instead, they used such critique to improve their artistic styles and perspectives.

Similarly, design thinking teams should regard critiques of their solutions as positive and constructive. They should not take negative comments about their proposed solutions personally. Instead, they should remember the adage, "The customer is not always right but always has a point."

In the evaluation phase, users are usually biased toward evaluating a new solution according to its similarity to existing products with which they are familiar. When asked to comment on a new solution, they may say something to the likes of, "The old one was better. I don't know why, but it was better!" To overcome this baby duck syndrome, the new solution should, if possible, inherit the main usage patterns of the existing product to which users are accustomed. In time, users will get used to the new solution. As Arthur Schopenhauer said, "Every truth passes through three stages before it is recognized. In the first it is ridiculed, in the second it is opposed, in the third it is regarded as self-evident."

During the evaluation phase, design thinking teams should prepare to deal with both yes-men and no-men. Yes-men are more dangerous than no-men because they are silent and friendly during evaluation sessions and are usually unhelpful in communicating the flaws of the proposed solution. Although no-men are usually regarded as extremists or troublemakers, they are generally more helpful in identifying what is missing or problematic about the proposed solution. If problems are not discussed and resolved at this early stage of the project, they will later necessitate high-cost efforts to fix the final product.

13. How Can You Benefit from Neuroaesthetics to Evoke Creativity at Design Thinking Workshops?

Organizations usually face three types of business challenges:

1. Known / Knowns: The root cause of the problem is definitely known.

2. Known / Unknowns: Possible root causes of the problem are known.

3. Unknown / Unknowns: The root cause of the business problem is definitely unknown.

Solving type 1 challenges requires empathy skills, whereas type 2 (complicated) challenges requires insightful thinking, and type 3 (complex) challenges requires creative thinking skills. Design thinking workshops are much more effective if they are designed to trigger these right-brain skills .

Academic research shows that artful thinking can invoke right-brain skills. Freud's journal *Imago*, for example, was one of the first efforts to combine art, neuroscience, and psychology. Nobel prize winner Professor Eric Richard Kandel, a neuroscientist at Columbia University, depicted the connection between abstract art and neuroscience. Using the works of artists such as Monet, Kandinsky, Mondrian, Pollock, de Kooning, and Rothko as examples, his reductionism theory demonstrates how the brain simplifies and solves a problem with minimal effort. Professor Semir Zeki, too, has contributed greatly to the field of Neuroaesthetics by illustrating the impact of artful experiences at the neurological level. He shows that the brain's emotional responses to artistic experiences are affected by the observer's empathy with the subject, the artist, and with his/herself. Studies in these fields help us to understand how artful thinking practices invoke the right-brain to empathize, yield insights through pattern recognition, associate unrelated subjects, and generate creativity.

In this context, artful thinking practices that evoke right-brain skills can be applied during design thinking workshops:

- Display concrete (known-knowns), semi-abstract (known-unknowns), and abstract (unknown-unknowns) paintings, and ask participants to interpret them. This exercise will invoke and help the right-brain to identify needs (known-knowns), insights (known-unknowns), and ideas (unknown-unknowns) during the workshop.

- Display several portraits, and ask participants to comment on the feelings of the characters portrayed in them. This artful thinking practice will encourage participants to better empathize during research activities.

Creativity is about associating internal thoughts with the environment around us. Author Steven Johnson argues that luck is on the side of brains that make connections. "What I'm saying," he claims, "is individuals have better ideas if they're connected to rich, diverse networks of other individuals. If you put yourself in an environment with lots of different perspectives, you yourself are going to have better, sharper, more original ideas. It's not that the network is smart."

Involvement in art activities and the attainment of artful thinking perspectives can help design thinking teams to better recognize patterns and make connections among the things they observe. According to mathematician and philosopher Alfred North Whitehead, "Art is the imposing of a pattern on experience, and our aesthetic enjoyment is recognition of the pattern." Poet and literary critic Herbert Read echoed this idea when he said, "Art is pattern informed by sensibility."

The study of art can help one to associate objects with artworks. This can occur, for example, when:

- the light and shadow effect on an object reminds you of a Rembrandt painting;

- you associate an extremely realistic painting with Caravaggio;

- a perfect combination of blue and yellow makes you think of van Gogh;

- you compare a sculpture to Rodin's artworks;

- your dreams invoke images of surrealist artists such as Salvador Dali and René Magritte;

- you think of Camille Corot and William Turner paintings upon gazing at a perfect landscape;

- you compare a perfect color combination to the works of Matisse.

- watching a ballet brings Edgar Degas to mind;

- being caught in the rain calls forth the paintings of Pissarro;

- you remember Giorgio de Chirico when you read philosophy;

- you recognize Piet Mondrian in minimalist geometrical shapes of blue, yellow, and red;

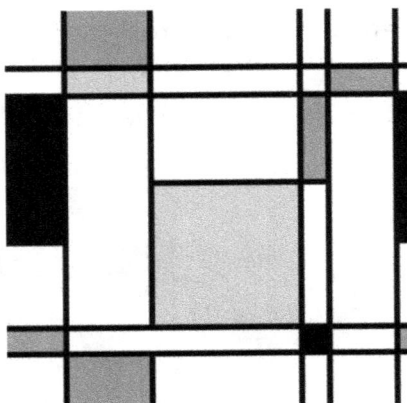

- the sight of a lonely woman reminds you of Edward Hopper's paintings;

- you couple the use of abstract figures with artists Wassily Kandinsky and Joan Miró.

The above examples are an indicator that your pattern-recognition skills are improving. This kind of recognition can lead to a better understanding of the deterministic cause-and-effect relationships among objects. When these skills are honed, you are better able to predict what will happen in certain conditions, an indicator of good intuition. Spinoza describes this as the third and most valuable type of knowledge. This same skill helps design thinking teams to explore the root causes of problems, identify insights, and generate creative ideas for solutions.

To invoke pattern recognition skills during design thinking workshops, the following artful thinking practice can be applied:

- First, summarize the main attributes of artworks belonging to specific art movements. Then, display various artworks and ask participants to associate them with art movements which use similar patterns. This practice will trigger participants' pattern recognition skills before they begin to group users' needs and expectations under specific insights.

The characteristics of the most famous art movements that may be used in this exercise are as follows:

- **Renaissance** artists placed great emphasis on realism through the use of perspective.

- **Rococo** painters used soft colors and curvy lines to create scenes of love, entertainment, and nature.

- **Romanticism**-period artists portrayed a nostalgia for the past.

- **Impressionism** focused on the effects of light and visual impressions of nature at certain times of the day. French artist Robert Delaunay call this "the birth of light in painting."

- **Fauvism** elicited emotion through the use of violent colors.

- **Expressionism** focused on the artist's emotion instead of a direct representation of nature.

- **Cubism** used geometric forms to simultaneously depict an object from many different angles.

- **Futurism** depicted the beauty of technological advances and machines.

- **Dada** was an "anti-art" movement.

- **Realism**-period artists painted scenes from everyday life.

- **Surrealism** focused on dreams and the subconscious and was influenced by Freud's theories on psychology.

- **Pop art** was the art of popular culture that characterized consumers, the globalization of pop music, and youth.

Another function of the brain that art can evoke is visual thinking. Abstract business and technology ideas do not create any value unless they are turned into concrete products, services, or solution concepts. By improving our visual thinking skills with artful thinking practices, we can more easily concretize ideas into tangible forms. Prototyping requires the application of these skills in design thinking workshops. Even Einstein once said, "If I can't picture it, I can't understand it." Visual thinking is like seeing with the mind. It is the ability to think through visuals and create images to express ideas. "The soul," said Aristo, "never thinks without a picture." From the earliest periods in human history, painting has been the most effective way to express thoughts and emotions through the integration of mind and soul. Leonardo da Vinci is the best example of this. In addition to his artworks, the prototypes that he designed for his inventions are also considered masterpieces. In 1994, Bill Gates paid $31 million for the Codex manuscript that included some of those prototypes.

To exercise workshop participants' right-brain skills in preparation for prototyping sessions, the following artful thinking practice can be applied:

- Ask participants to express a feeling (such as the experience of living in a crowded city) by drawing or painting it, and then ask other participants to interpret it. This practice will trigger their visual thinking skills before they begin conceptualizing ideas via prototyping.

According to Banksy, "Art should comfort the disturbed and disturb the comfortable.' In the same vein, artful practices not only invoke participants' right-brain skills but also keep them more active and sharp throughout the workshop.

14. What if Picasso Had Been a Design Thinker?

Ultimately, creativity is a skill that is best attained during childhood. As Picasso said: "Every child is an artist. The problem is how to remain an artist once we grow up." It has been proven that introducing liberal arts to children at an early age significantly enhances their creative capacity. However, most countries' educational systems lack this dimension. Children do not usually have the chance to integrate creativity and analytical skills.

People missing this opportunity in childhood should at least be introduced to liberal arts in later stages of their lives. Design thinking teams can unlock their creative genius by spending the time to analyze and understand the work of artists such as cubist Pablo Picasso and Georges Braque; impressionists such as Claude Monet and Paul Cezanne; expressionists such as Vincent van Gogh, Edvard Munch, Mark Rothko, and Wassily Kandinsky; and surrealists such as Salvador Dali, Giorgio de Chirico, and René Magritte; all of whom innovated creative ways to express their ideas.

Among all artists, Paul Cezanne is recognized as the most avant-garde, as he changed the course of modern art. Émile Zola once said that he was a genius ahead of his time. Even great artists such as Matisse and Picasso regarded Cezanne as "the father of us all." Cezanne once said, "With an apple I want to astonish Paris." Cezanne formed a new revolutionary approach by restructuring the relationship between form and color and created a new visual language that conveyed emotions to the viewer.

Fauvist artist Henri Matisse defined composition as "The art of arranging in a decorative manner the diverse elements at the painter's command to express his feelings." Thanks to new composition techniques, new color palettes, and simplified forms, he managed to create positive energy for the viewers of his artworks . He always advised young artists to make up their own rules and create "the new" after they master the basics.

Andy Warhol, another avant-garde artist, led the pop art movement and created a new way of thinking in art. He once said that "Being good in business is the most fascinating kind of art. Making money is art and working is art and good business is the best art." He inspired businesspeople to view their businesses like a piece of art. We remember his quote especially when we work on "the new" business and technology solutions by using business model "canvas" and value proposition "canvas." Simultaneously a businessman, he achieved scalability in art making using new techniques such as serigraph and silkscreens. He called his studio "the factory" and motivated art lovers to visit and contribute to his artworks with their ideas and even brushstrokes. For exposure to different styles, he collaborated with artists like Basquiat and, thanks to his close relationships with celebrities of the time, created great marketing hype. With all of these "new" ways of making and promoting art, he became one of the few artists who made a fortune before he died.

Thanks to his development of new composing techniques, Johann Sebastian Bach is regarded as one of the greatest musicians of all time. He invented a universal form of musical grammar with a mathematical logic that helped musicians create complex musical compositions that otherwise could only have been mastered by geniuses such as Mozart and Beethoven. Even computers and amateur musicians can now compose and play music based on the form of musical grammar that Bach created.

Miles Davis was another musician who was always looking for "the new." In order to foster improvisation, he discouraged his jazz band from practicing before performances. This risky approach allowed them to create new and unexpected compositions. Improvisation is the act of generating on-the-fly creative solutions without a lot of preparation. It is the ability to perform spontaneously and is an effective way to encourage creativity. Improvisation skills can best be improved by becoming involved in artful thinking activities such as creative drama and jazz music.

Analyzing the works and stories of avant-garde artists such as Cezanne, Picasso, Matisse, Andy Warhol, Bach, and Miles Davis can help design thinking teams improve their creative potential by looking beyond the frame in an avant-garde style.

Walter Gropius, founder of the Bauhaus school, was one of the most prominent people to showing how artistic perspectives contribute to design thinking. His goal was "to create a new guild of craftsmen without the class distinctions which raise an arrogant barrier between craftsman and artist." Bauhaus was established in Germany as an art school that combined art and craft and revolutionized product design.

It used the slogan *"Art into Industry"* and brought creative expression to product design. Its mission included the "vision of unification of the arts through craft." Artists such as Paul Klee and Wassily Kandinsky contributed to Bauhaus as instructors. The curriculum included workshops on painting, sculpture, cabinetmaking, textiles, metalworking, and typography. The vision and working principles of the Bauhaus school have long been a role model for design and innovation teams.

In recent years, the majority of innovative companies and leading universities such as Harvard and MIT have applied "artful thinking" to improve whole-brain skills by embedding art into professional, academic, and personal life. In academia, the STEM system (science, technology, engineering, and maths) turned into the STEAM system (science, technology, engineering, art, and maths). Maker fairs all around the world began to incorporate art into their events in order to foster creative thinking.

Artful thinking allows us to view business and personal life from different perspectives. What if famous artists such as Picasso, Da Vinci, Dali, and Van Gogh were business and technology professionals? As French novelist and critic Marcel Proust said, "The real voyage of discovery consists not in seeking new landscapes, but in having new eyes." Artful thinking helps us see the world with these new eyes and use this increased awareness and mindfulness in the creation of innovative business and technology solutions. With this aim in mind, art fairs in Silicon Valley exhibiting important artworks of the twentieth and twenty-first centuries are organized in collaboration with the world's most respected galleries and art institutions.

Many of the cofounders and CEOs of the world's most innovative companies in Silicon Valley have been liberal arts graduates who integrated art with business and technology and led their companies to create innovative products. Norio Ohga, for instance, the former president and chairman of Sony Corporation and the inventor of the compact disk (CD), was a graduate of the Tokyo National University of Fine Arts and Music. Steve Jobs also took many liberal arts courses and once said, "It is technology married with liberal arts, married with the humanities that yields the results that make our hearts sing." Therefore, one of the most effective steps that companies can take to unlock creativity, foster innovation, and develop delightful solutions that touch the hearts of people is the application of design thinking methodology and an artful thinking mindset. By doing so, they can replace shallow organizational mindsets with deeper ones, resulting in improved emotional intelligence and creative empowerment

15. How Can Inspiration from Nature Help You Become a More Creative Design Thinker?

Illustrated by ancient cave drawings, nature has always been one of the primary inspirations for creative people. The story of Renaissance artist Giotto di Bondone is a perfect example of this. When Giotto was a child living in the village of Vespigano, Italy, he drew animal figures on rocks. When Florentine painter Cimabue once visited the same village, he happened across Giotto's rock drawings of sheep. Cimabue was attracted to Giotto's style and convinced the boy's father to allow him to take Giotto to Florence as his apprentice. After working with his master for only a couple of years, Giotto began to gain a reputation as an artistic genius.

Inspiration from nature can be observed not only in art but also in almost every industry. Nature, itself, is in a continuous creative process. To be innovative is to observe nature's creative artifacts and use them to meet people's specific needs.

Famous architect Antoni Gaudi is one of the most prominent examples of this kind of innovation. When Gaudi was a child, he suffered from poor health, which prevented him from attending school. As a result, he spent most of his time in nature, which inspired his design approach. His philosophy that "The great book always open and which we should make an effort to read, is that of Nature" motivated him to design buildings in an "organic style," which later became an important standard in architecture.

Steve Jobs is another important figure who was inspired by nature. He revolutionized the high-tech industry by positioning people's natural behaviors at the center of the product-development process. This approach led to the innovation of the most usable consumer electronics products ever created. Jobs' objective was to create natural-born users of his products. Now, even children can use his company's phones and touch pads with gestures mimicking their natural behaviors. This new design approach allowed his company to become one of the best performers in the high-tech industry.

16. Is Design Thinking Magic?

Every organization's top two agenda items are related to being more innovative in:

- creating products, technologies, services, and spaces that people love; and

- overcoming complex business, technological, and social problems with new ideas, processes, and business models.

Organizations search for magical ways of achieving these two objectives. They attend conferences and purchase trend reports or invest considerable time and budget in efforts to apply trendy approaches which do not lead to expected results. In turn, low ROIs (return on investments) cause a huge amount of sunk costs for these organizations.

The use of methods as a magic cure-all is one of the main causes of institutional failure. Methods are like wizards, not magicians. They can only help organizations do their work more efficiently through the use of systematic approach and practical toolsets. Similarly, design thinking is not magical. But it can help organizations create innovate solutions by applying a human centered, collaborative, and experimental mindset.

This mindset results in:

- **Accelerated Decision Making:** In classical product and service development approaches, people periodically gather together in 1-2 hour meetings, with limited dedication. Sometimes it takes months to decide on a new solution. Teams applying design thinking methodology, however, hold workshops to focus on generating innovative solution ideas within a limited time frame. As the saying goes, "creativity loves constraints." This dedicated approach, in other words, accelerates the decision-making process in the creation of innovative solution ideas for specific business challenges.

- **Collaborative Decision Making:** In design thinking workshops, multidisciplinary teams from different organizational units meet to find solutions for other departments' challenges. They apply collaborative techniques such as affinity diagrams and brain-dumps. Over time, this problem-solving and decision-making approach leads to the formation of a more collaborative company culture.

- **Effective Decision Making:** Design thinking workshops use solution ideas to evaluate prototypes. In this way, customer feedback can be gathered more quickly, and the effectiveness of solution ideas can be tested efficiently and inexpensively.

- **Insightful Decision Making:** Design thinking workshop teams focus on generating actionable insights by using techniques such as mind mapping and affinity diagrams. This insight-based approach increases the chances of generating more disruptive innovation ideas.

- **Systematic Decision Making:** Design thinking promotes creativity rather than imagination. Each idea generated during the workshops is evaluated and prioritized according to its value proposition and implementation difficulty. Then, selected ideas are prototyped as a solution concept. This systematic decision-making process prevents the loss of high value ideas generated during the workshops. In other words, it turns "valuable" ideas into "important" and tangible solutions that have an impact.

After holding several design thinking workshops, the design thinking mindset and empowered decision-making process becomes a cultural style. As Coco Chanel said "Fashion fades, only style remains the same." So even if a company replaces design thinking with another approach, it will still continue to benefit from its cultural heritage.

17. What Kinds of Challenges Can You Solve by Applying Design Thinking?

Steve Jobs believed that design is as much about function as about looks. "Most people," he said, make the mistake of thinking design is what it looks like. People think it's this veneer – that the designers are handed this box and told, "Make it look good!" That's not what we think design is. It's not just what it looks like and feels like. Design is how it works."

In the same respect, design thinking is not about pixels, look, feel, or visual aesthetics. It is a method that benefits from the designer's approach to solve challenges at strategic, tactical, and operational levels.

As outcome of design thinking workshops, a physical object (such as a new product, technology, or space) or an intangible concept (such as a new service, process, experience, or business / operating model) can be developed in response to a particular challenge.

In most organizations, design thinking projects are only initiated to develop innovative customer-facing products or services because they directly impact sales, profitability, customer satisfaction, and loyalty. The return on investment (ROI) of these projects is usually very high. However, organizations should not underestimate the value of design thinking in overcoming challenges related to enterprise processes, such as human resources and supply chain management. Applying design thinking to solve problems associated with these processes may bring huge cost-savings because of improved efficiency and productivity. In other words, design thinking is also effective in solving backstage challenges, as it is in solving customer-facing front stage challenges. Below are some front and backstage examples of challenges that can be solved at design thinking workshops:

- How might we retain customers who prefer non-traditional digital competitors?

- How might we reach young customers by changing our go-to-market strategy?

- How might we improve our orientation and onboarding processes to shorten the adaptation period for new hires?

- How might we initiate online sales while avoiding conflicts with our traditional dealers?

- How might we re-energize our company by fostering a more creative and collaborative organizational culture ?

- How might we create team spirit among our employees located in different cities?

- How might we reach out to the best university talent before our competitors?

Coco Chanel said, "In order to be irreplaceable one must always be different." This "difference" that is created during design thinking workshops not only help organizations solve today's challenges, but also prepares them for the future by mitigating the risks of:

- being a commoditized business,

- becoming a monotone, silo-based organization,

- being unable to adapt to new technologies, and

- being replaced by non-traditional competitors.

As Albert Einstein said, "Insanity is doing the same things over and over again and expecting different results." Organizations avoid this pitfall by applying design thinking to solve challenges and awaken an innovative spirit. However, they should still start small by first practicing design thinking on relatively easy challenges and then applying this methodology to solve more challenging problems. The "forming, storming, norming, and performing" model of group development that Bruce Tuckman proposes can be used to implement new methodologies. All organizations experience each of these four consecutive phases when a new methodology is applied. When design thinking teams confront barriers raised by peers and upper management, they should not simply give up. Instead, they should do their best to obtain buy-in from others. When they feel demotivated, they should remember that "it is not the strength of waves that shapes the rocks, but it is their persistence."

18. How Can Design Thinking Be Used to Create a More Innovative Organization?

Most companies apply idea pools as a way to foster innovation. They periodically ask employees to post their creative ideas to an idea pool on the intranet. These ideas are then evaluated by a dedicated group of people in the organization. This approach, however, is usually ineffective due to two main drawbacks:

1- No Voice of Customer

Customers are not involved during idea generation. Instead, ideas are generated based solely on employees' perspectives.

2- Individualistic

In this approach, employees whose ideas are selected as the most innovative are rewarded. This hurts the spirit of collaboration within the organization. It also sometimes results in conflicts of ownership and copyright problems. Additionally, employees may not share their ideas, keeping them for their own future start-up initiatives.

Most companies have begun to apply design thinking to mitigate these drawbacks of the classical approach. Compared to idea pools, design thinking is customer-centric and collaborative.

✓ Customer-centricity

Design thinking focuses on formulating solutions that best meet customer needs. Products and services are regarded not as final objectives, but as tools used to meet people's needs. In other words, they are developed by listening to the voice of the customer. To achieve this objective, customers are directly involved in the research and evaluation sessions of design thinking workshops. All of the techniques applied during workshops (including personas, journey maps, mind maps, empathy maps, and value proposition canvas) are customer-centric.

✓ Collaboration

Compared to classical idea pooling methods, design thinking workshops generate ideas gleaned from groups of people rather than from individuals. Multidisciplinary teams from different departments meet to develop innovative solutions by applying collaborative idea-generation techniques.

Rather than being an alternative approach, however, design thinking can be considered complementary to idea pools. Although design thinking is much more effective, idea pools are still useful in providing a medium for all employees to share innovative ideas. Organizations can integrate idea pooling and design thinking approaches by following these steps:

1. Review all ideas submitted to the idea pool.

2. Categorize these ideas based on the problems and opportunities they address.

3. Convert these categories into challenge statements in the form of HMW (how might we) questions.

4. Conduct design thinking workshops to address each of these challenges.

19. How Can You Use Design Thinking to Reenergize Your Organization?

The size of a company cannot be measured by the financial capital on its balance sheet or the number of its employees; it is beyond these figurative measures. The real size of a company depends on its number of happy and positive employees because it is only they who can turn the financial capital of the company into innovative products and delightful experiences. Only happy employees can create new stories and unlock a company's real potential. In the majority of companies, though, unmotivated employees usually outnumber positive and energetic employees. The resulting negative energy dampens the positive energy of those who are motivated.

"The next big thing" determining a company's success will be not only digital transformation but also a new way of thinking that will transform an organization's energy. Positive organizational energy is not only a matter of compensation, promotions, or playful offices. It is much more about an organization's aura, which is generated by people creating "the new" as "a team."

If always working on individual, routine tasks in a silo-based business environment, even the most self-motivated people can become sad and depressed. Mihaly Csikszentmihalyi's model summarizes this situation in a very elegant way.

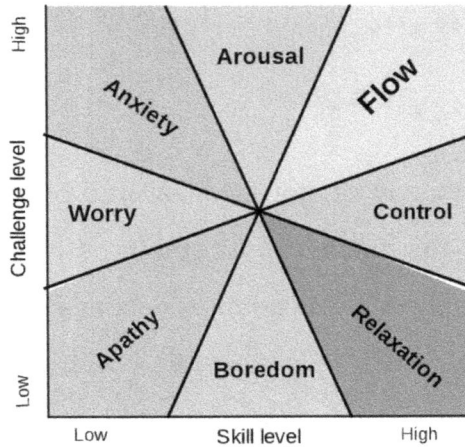

Achieving the state of "flow" (the happy, intuitive, and creative side) necessitates two things: having challenges ("the new") that make you release dopamine and having the skills to help you convert that dopamine's energy into actionable ideas and results. However, employees may not have enough opportunity in their own business domain to take part in innovative projects designed to create "the new." Even if they do have such opportunities, they may lack the skill set needed for the specific project. To overcome this dual problem, most companies have begun to apply design thinking as a new way of thinking.

People from different organizational units gather at design thinking workshops to create innovative solutions for other departments' challenges. A marketing department challenge, for instance, involves not only marketing employees but also employees from IT, finance, human resources, sales, and other departments. In this manner, each design thinking workshop provides the opportunity to work on different challenges, and the organization can leverage the competencies of employees who have different skill sets.

Design thinking workshops also help companies achieve equal participation by involving people from different levels of the organization. CEOs, managers, experienced employees, and new-hire employees sit around the same tables and focus on solving challenges without hierarchical limitations. This helps companies optimize the power interest grid by making powerful people (executives) more interested and interested people (employees) more powerful.

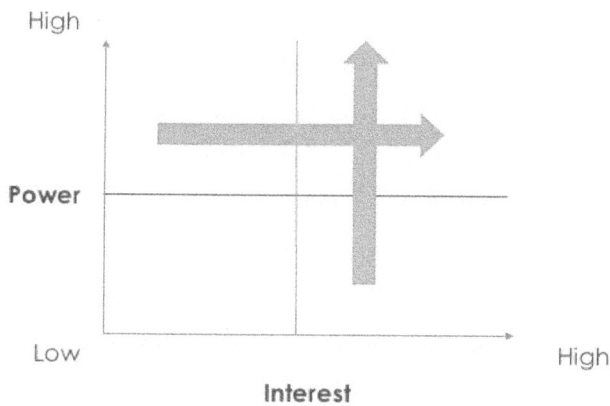

Amy Brann's book *Engaged* uses a neuroscience perspective to describe how collective decision making can be achieved. She argues that group flow is possible in the existence of shared clear goals, good communication, equal participation, and a sense of autonomy. Inheriting all these characteristics, design thinking is a perfect way for companies to move their organization into the "state of flow," to foster creativity, and to increase social capital.

Famous artist Joseph Beuys said that only individual creativity could transform society. He believed that unlocking the creative potential of every individual is the only revolutionary force that can protect society from the negative consequences of pure profit-oriented capitalism. When he said that "everyone is an artist," he meant that everyone can apply artistic practices, whether it be at work, at home, or any other everyday context.

20. How Can You Use Design Thinking to Create Better Employee Experience (EX)?

Design Thinking is a methodology that unleashes its real potential when applied by companies who redefined the meaning of an organization.

As beautifully described in Jim Whitehurst's book *The Open Organization*, only organizations with an authentic purpose can truly connect with and inspire passion among their employees and customers. Such companies measure their value not only in terms of solid figures (such as revenue or profit) but also in terms of the social value they create for their employees, customers, and the public. As Theodore Roosevelt Malloch said, "A visionary company understands profit in the way that the biologist understands oxygen, not the goal of life but the thing without which there is no life."

Similarly, visionary, open organizations make their employees feel that they are contributing to real things, not just numbers. They are not motivated by numeric key performance indicators but by the experience of creating value for those in their impact zone. Artist Mark Rothko echoed the same sentiment when he said that "A painting is not a picture of an experience; it is an experience." Health institutions, for instance, should focus not only on revenue but also on how many of their patients are recovering. In the same manner, financial institutions should focus not only on the size of their mortgage loans but also on how many young couples they helped to buy their first homes. And insurance companies should focus not only on the size of their policy portfolios but also on the number of customers they assisted after or helped protect from accidents.

Saint Francis of Assisi said that "He who works with his hands is a labourer. He who works with his hands and his head is a craftsman. He who works with his hands and his head and his heart is an artist." People feel like artists in open organizations where they are:

- having good moments with colleagues

- socializing while working

- celebrating success and confronting failure as a team

- leaving their routine and taking initiative

- maintaining a creative balance of order vs. disorder

- working in a playful and energetic environment

Incorporating all of these factors, design thinking is a perfect match for open organizations, and open organizations are the perfect environments to unleash the power of design thinking. The human-centric and insight-driven approach of design thinking can be used to create great employee experience. In one of our projects, our EX team facilitated a design thinking workshop for a finance institution. The challenge was: "How might we shorten the adaptation duration (onboarding) of new hires to the company?" During the research phase, the team interviewed candidates and employees and applied the mind mapping technique to explore the factors that negatively impacted new hires' adaptation to the organization. Mind mapping revealed that employees experienced a significant sense of uncertainty during the period between the job offer date and the first day of the work. Because this feeling of uncertainty persisted, it took a longer period of time for new hires to adapt. As H.P. Lovecraft said, "The oldest and strongest emotion of mankind is fear, and the oldest and strongest kind of fear is fear of the unknown." Based on this insight, the team created a digital solution that would orient new hires before their first day at work. The team used gamification to create the new concept, which increases the desirability and usability of the solution. After implementing this digital solution, the company shortened its onboarding time from months to weeks.

21. How Can You Use Design Thinking to Create Better Customer Experience (CX)?

In Plato's famous allegory, a group of people are chained to a cave and can only see the shadows on the inner wall they are facing. Those people would think that the figures appearing on the wall are real and would not understand the real causes of the shadows. They would consider their experience in the cave as the real world.

In the majority of companies, the innovation and design process is conducted in offices similar to modern caves. The teams working with a "what if we were the customers" approach base their design decisions on shadows similar to those in Plato's cave. These shadows are the data mined from CRM (customer relationship management) systems and survey-based market research.

Data-driven methods can help identify customer behaviors but cannot necessarily interpret the reasons for those behaviors. The shadows may reveal customers' needs and pain points but cannot interpret their root causes. In other words, you can't capture customer insights that arise mainly from people's emotions and motivations.

Design thinking workshops reveal that innovative products and services that truly satisfy customers and bring a "wow" effect can only be created when the ideas are based on customer insights. Ideas that may create excitement in the office are not always welcomed by customers. The number one objective of design thinking teams, therefore, should be to generate insights by listening to the voice of end customers prior to and during the workshops. The aura of ideas depends on the depth of the insights they are based on. To capture deep insights, design thinking teams should focus not only on what customers do, say, or think, but also on what they feel. Empathy mapping, mind mapping, and affinity diagrams are practical techniques which help teams to capture deep insights. Below is an example for this insight-based innovation approach:

ArtBizTech is a multi-disciplinary group of people including business professionals, technology specialists, psychologists, designers, and artists that help companies generate creative ideas; develop innovative products, technologies, and services; and solve all types of business challenges by applying Design Thinking Methodology and Artful Thinking Perspectives. In one of their assignments, the ArtBizTech team conducted a design thinking workshop at a hospital to solve the following challenge: "How might we create a relaxing launch area experience for patients?". The team applied the empathy mapping technique to learn what the target groups thought and felt at the start of their journey in the hospital. Then, hospital psychologists, together with the ArtBizTech team, worked together on an affinity diagram to explore the patterns among customers' thoughts and feelings. One insight the team identified was that "when they step inside the hospital, people not only expect to feel relaxation and revival but also reassured that the hospital employs the latest technology." The team brain-dumped many ideas that might create these feelings upon arrival to the hospital. The "wow" idea involved displaying a neuroaesthetics-inspired digital artwork in the entrance hall. Being digital, it would evoke the spirit of advanced technology, while at the same time inspiring the feeling of relaxation and peace through its use of images, colors, and forms. The artists from NOHLAB, along with ArtBiztech's technology experts, the Bang.Prix team's curators and the Bang.Neuro team's art directors, worked together for three months to create a huge digital artwork called "Ab-ı Hayat," meaning "the water of life." It is now displayed via 48 HD video walls on three floors of the hospital. In addition to creating a new dimension of time and space, it also suggests an experience of healing and recovery for hospital visitors. Since its installation, it has become the corporate identity of the hospital, and visitors often stop to take photos in front of it .

22. How Can Design Thinking Help You Succeed in Digital Transformation?

In recent years, digital technologies such as artificial intelligence, robotics, IOT (internet of things), augmented reality, virtual reality, and blockchain have become a part of daily life. This is partially thanks to a substantial increase in the processing power of computers, advances in big data and cloud technologies, and the proliferation of wireless networks.

Digital transformation has become the number-one agenda item of executives, and companies spend millions of dollars on digital transformation projects. However, the ROI related to such digitalization efforts is often disappointing. Only a small number of organizations succeed in leveraging the power of digital technologies, and most create digital products and services in which target users have no interest.

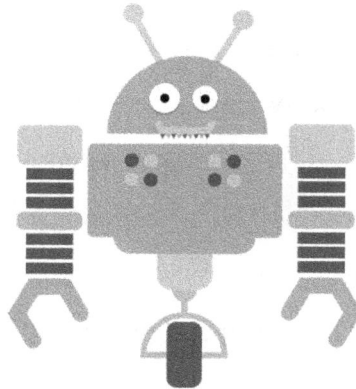

Copernicus said, "What appear to us as motions of the sun arise not from its motion but from the motion of the earth and our sphere, with which we revolve about the sun like any other planet." After the acceptance of Copernicus's theory, people understood for the first time that the sun was the center of the planets in the solar system. This was a paradigm shift in the mindset of those who had envisioned the earth as the center of the universe. This new way of thinking hastened developments in science. A similar paradigm shift must occur in the mindsets of those responsible for digital transformation, replacing the shallow, technology-centric mindset with a more human-centric one.

Organizations must realize that because innovation is a matter of formulating solutions that best meet people's needs, it cannot only be achieved at the technical level. Therefore, digital technologies should be regarded as tools rather than final objectives. As Steve Jobs suggested, "You have got to start with the customer experience and work back toward the technology—not the other way around." He also said that "True innovation comes from recognizing an unmet need and designing a creative way to fill it." As a human-centered methodology, design thinking is very helpful in realizing this approach. Design thinking workshops that are organized as part of digital transformation projects use a customer-centric approach to define challenge statements. An example of one such statement might be: "How might we use digitalization to create attract, engage, and retain customers?" A challenge statement defined by a technology-centric approach, on the other hand, might be: "How might our company apply the most recent digital technologies?" Workshops participants should not be directed to think about digitalization until customer needs and insights are identified. After customer insights are interpreted, facilitators should ask participants to begin ideating creative digital solutions. Offering a brief introduction to digital technologies before ideation sessions can be helpful, as some participants' knowledge may be limited. Digitalization ideas should then be prioritized as:

- "wows": high value digitalization ideas that can be implemented without excessive resources,

- "hows": digitalization ideas for the future, and

- "nows": quick wins.

Upon prioritization, the selected digitalization ideas should be prototyped to get customer feedback. By applying this customer-centric and insight-driven approach, digital solution ideas that create an aura for target users can be generated successfully.

Insurance is one industry for which there is fierce price competition and high risk of commoditization. Ever changing customer patterns in other industries also put extra pressure on the players of the insurance industry. The proliferation of autonomous cars and ride-sharing, for example, raises questions of who to insure, how to insure, and at what price to insure. To address these challenges, visionary insurance companies differentiate themselves by designing better customer experiences. The most successful are customer-centric companies that can identify customer insights and use digital technologies to turn them into great experiences.

Insurance companies have found the following insight-based digital solutions to be highly effective:

- An insurance company designed a peer-to-peer (P2P) solution which allows friends and families to apply for group plans at discounted rates. Every additional peer connection brings extra discounts. Customers receive refunds if they don't file claims during any given year. This P2P digital insurance solution was created based on two insights:

- "People elicit advice from families and colleagues before purchasing insurance policies."

- "People always fear that insurance companies are overcharging them, even if they are loyal customers."

- An insurance company targeting young customers created a mobile application that speeds up the insurance application and claim process to seconds. Thanks to artificial intelligence technology at the back-end, customers can apply through a chatbot and file a claim by video chat. The solution was created on the insight that:

  - "Young customers find the application and claim process to be bureaucratic, complex, and time-consuming."

As a result of success in intersecting customer insights through effective digital technologies, the company became the number one preference for young customers in a very short span of time.

- A home insurance company created a product that was based on the insight that:

  - "People expect to be protected more than to be insured."

The insurance company provides its customers with a smart home system when they purchase an insurance policy. The system's IOT-based sensors send notifications to the customer's mobile phone in case of a fire, theft, or flood. It also makes the claim payment in case there is damage to the home. Another insurance company who captured a similar insight inserts a mobile device in your car that includes GPS and sensor technologies. It warns the customer in case he/she exceeds speed limits. Based on the sensor data received, it automatically calls an ambulance if it detects that the driver has had an accident. In this way, it not only insures but also protects the customer.

- A health insurance company created a digital loyalty program which tracks customers' activities and rewards them for each action that is good for their health, such as buying fruits or purchasing gym memberships. The mobile application or wearable device even counts the number of steps the customer takes each day . Based on the big data it receives, customers can earn discounts on their next policy renewal. This digital solution was created on the insight that:

    o "People expect a more positive, assuring relationship from their insurance companies."

- One insurance company moved with the following insight:

    o "People perceive insurance as a necessary evil rather than a social good."

When customers apply for a policy through the mobile application, they select a nonprofit organization that they care about. At the end of the year, the insurance company pays back a portion of the unclaimed money to the nonprofit that the customer chose during the application process. In doing so, they bring a social barrier to fraud and create a positive bond with their customers.

- An insurance company benefits from big data technologies in order to follow digital footprints and prevent fraud. In a car accident claim, for example, the system detected that the claim owners were friends on social media and automatically sent the case for further investigation. Another insurance company uses big data technologies to identify people with similar health problems and offers them group insurance policies at discounted rates.

23. How Can Your Company Use Design Thinking to Create a New Story?

When Picasso was asked which period was his best (such as his blue or cubism periods), he said it is "the next one." The Keytorc technology company used this quote as inspiration in creating its new story.

The company was established in 2005 as a startup that aimed to help companies by outsourcing their IT (information technology) resources, which ranged from coding to software testing. To test their business model, Keytorc founders decided to take part in a regional IT fair. Although the fair would consume a considerable part of the company's budget, it was an important opportunity to listen to the voice of potential clients. On the very first day, the fair produced two key insights:

- Keytorc founders realized that they had a focus problem. Visitors to the Keytorc expressed confusion concerning the IT outsourcing services presented in the marketing materials.

- Fifty percent of interested visitors asked for more information about the outsourcing of software testing services.

Based on these two insights, Keytorc founders decided to test the impact of positioning the company as a focused team that worked solely on software testing. On the second day of the fair, Keytorc stand visitors were welcomed with a huge poster reading: "Your Software is **Tested by Keytorc.**" Compared to the previous day, the number of visitors increased exponentially. Thanks to its focused strategy, the company acquired its first client and established many leads.

After the fair, the code of Keytorc's DNA was defined as: "Focus and Create with Customers." Until now, the company has served more than 1,500 clients from a wide range of industries, listed as one of the 20 leading testing providers, and been one of the finalists of the Devops Industry and European Software Testing Awards.

In alignment with its focused and customer-centric strategy, the company continuously monitored customer needs and insights in the market. In 2007, it established a BA-Works team which provides business analysis services, and in 2009, it established a UXservices team which provides user experience design, service design, customer experience design, user research and usability testing services.

Over time, the Keytorc, BA-Works, and UXservices teams began to share their knowledge and experience with the industry by organizing international conferences and publishing books which are listed in Amazon Best Seller categories.

In 2017, after Keytorc, BA-Works, and UXservices teams began to function as separate entities, the HR team applied design thinking methodology in order to address the concern that the three teams were no longer working as a unified team, even though they were working in complementary areas.

The challenge statement was defined as follows: "How might we create an open organization in which employees from Keytorc, BA-Works, and UXservices can act as one team?"

At the research phase, the project team spoke with all employees working at headquarters and different client locations. After analyzing the research results on empathy maps and mind maps, the design thinking team identified the following insights:

- There is a need for a common authentic purpose representing the singular passion of all team members, regardless of their team or role in the company.

- The connection of outsource teams to the company is stronger when they meet with other colleagues.

- All employees appreciated the innovative spirit of the company and wanted to be an integral part of it.

Based on these insights, the design thinking team organized a brain-dump session with employees from each team to generate creative solution ideas. A conceptual HR strategy was designed during the workshop.

Following "Design Thinking" efforts, the company then engaged in "Design Doing" by acknowledging that action speaks louder than words. The results of their efforts were:

- A common purpose was defined: "We are inspired people creating "the new" as "a team.""

- The headquarters of the company was moved to a larger office, where all team members working in different locations could meet and socialize together. Artists were consulted to help create an inspiring and positive aura for the new "Design Thinking + Doing Studio."

- A Talent 4.0 program was initiated. It aimed to inspire employees with different perspectives such as artful thinking, behavior economics, and psychology. The program sessions were a perfect opportunity for employees to socialize and get to know one another.

- A social responsibility project aiming to help children realize their dreams was also initiated. It was identified at a separate design thinking workshop with the involvement of all employees and created high engagement.

- Working groups were formed to create "the new" for the company. Employees were given the opportunity to work with different team members in order to create "the new" together.

- While the company applied an "outside in" design approach which involved customers in the design of every new service, it applied an "inside out" marketing strategy. Rather than posting generic ads to social media accounts, the company began sharing happy team "moments" of creating "the new" as "a team".

- Email groups were formed so that all team members could share their tips and experiences with other colleagues.

- Regardless of seniority status, all team members were encouraged to share their experiences in specific domains and technologies by posting articles to the company's blog.

- A separate hi-tech team was established within the company to assist all team members in projects requiring experience in digital technologies such as artificial intelligence and RPA (robotics process automation).

- As Peter Drucker said, "Lead people, manage things." The roles of senior employees were redefined to promote leadership rather than management. New tools were implemented to manage things more efficiently.

With their new story, the company began to experience "the next big thing" — positive energy— in an open organization. This positive energy became the fuel to inspire the team to create "the new" as "a team."

24. How Can You Use Design Thinking to Create a Bestseller Product?

In 2013, the BA-Works team decided to write a book that would allow them to share their experience and know-how with people from all around the world working in the field of business analysis. The team formed a working group that was responsible for content creation, publishing, and marketing of the book. After nine months of hardwork, the book was ready to be published.

Unfortunately, the team was disappointed with the first print's number of sales. The book sold only a few copies in a three-month period. The team was confident in the quality of content but not in the positioning and marketing of the book. As a result, the BA-Works team decided to apply design thinking methodology to solve this challenge.

The group working on the book had previously neglected to gather feedback from target readers during the preparation of the first print but now decided to talk to as many business analysts (BAs) as possible. The target reader groups were classified under two personas: BAs with less than three years of experience, and experienced BAs who have team leadership or BA management roles in their companies. Group members targeted those who participated in BA-Works's training courses for interviews. The points raised by interviewees were then grouped and analyzed in affinity diagrams. As a result, the working group identified the following insights:

- While the experienced group was more interested in receiving mentorship, BAs with less than three years of experience were mainly interested in learning about BA methodologies and techniques.

- The target users noted that they preferred short books which they could easily carry with them on short business trips.

- The title of the first print was: *Thales Way of Software Requirements Management*. Almost all research participants said that this title gave them the impression of an old-fashioned book containing old-school knowledge.

- When asked about their search criteria for BA books, research participants said that they typed either "business analysis book" or "business analyst book" as keywords. When asked why they included the word "book" as a keyword, they explained that it resulted in a narrower list, as there are often many categories in online stores.

Based on these insights, the book working group reworked the cover, content, and title of the book. Rather than adding new sections, parts of the content were removed to make it more concise and easy to read. Their decision to simplify the content was inspired by two main sources: novelist Antoine de Saint Exupery, who said that "A designer knows he has achieved perfection not when there is nothing left to add, but when there is nothing left to take away," and Auguste Rodin, who once said, "I choose a block of marble and chop off whatever I don't need."

After their design thinking and design doing efforts, the BA-Works team published the book with a new title *Business Analyst*'s Mentor Book.

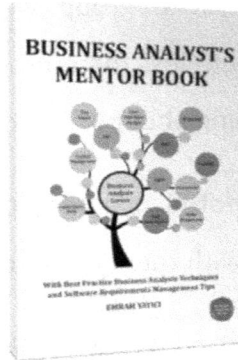

The team excitedly monitored the sales figures of the new book. After a few days, the sales graphics skyrocketed. The book's sales increased exponentially each following day. Within a couple of months, the book was listed as the best seller in the Amazon System Analysis and Design category.

As book reviews began to appear, the team felt more motivated because they could see that the insights they identified during their design thinking efforts had been successful. Some of the reviews were:

- "Really great book. As they say in the auto commercials: 'everything you need and nothing you don't.' Clear, concise, to the point, yet covering a lot of territory."

- "I have read this book during my 4 hour flight and enjoyed it. It is full of insights for all levels of business analysts."

- "I really, really, really wish I had this book when I was first starting my BA career. And yes, it is that good."

Not all of the reviews were so positive, of course:

- "It would be better if it includes examples for BA in context for my business."

- "It's about practical day-to-day philosophy for BA. No tools information here."

Readers posting negative comments expected more information and examples about business analysis tools and techniques. The BA-Works team therefore decided to leverage this insight in creating their next book.

In 2015, the team published the *Business Analysis Methodology Book*, which focused on business analysis tools and techniques. A real-life case study with sample project documents and diagrams was also included to more practically explain the methodologies, tools, and techniques. Within a few months, this book was also listed as one of the bestselling books in the Amazon System Analysis and Design and Consulting categories.

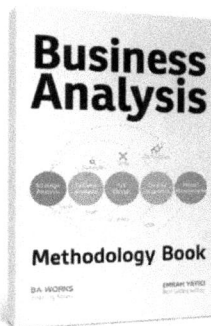

Since their publication, these two books have sold thousands of copies in more than 20 countries. Their success accelerated the BA-Works team's efforts at becoming a global, rather than just a regional thought-leader. It also helped the team to become an open organization motivated to not only create "the new" but also to share it.

25. How Can You Use Design Thinking to Create a Social Platform?

During their innovation consulting engagements with organizations from various industries, the ArtBizTech team has always acknowledged the importance of non-linear thinking skills in creating innovative solutions.

Non-linear thinking is a must-have rather than a nice-to-have because innovation can only be achieved by sensing the following things:

- Foresights: "non-linear shifts in the market" such as non-traditional competitors, new distribution channels, and disrupting technologies.

- Insights: "non-linear root causes of people's needs and expectations."

The ArtBizTech team decided to begin an initiative that aimed to help business professionals in improving their non-linear thinking skills. ArtBizTech organized a design thinking workshop involving professionals from various industries and domains. The following insights were captured:

- People mostly employ the same strategies of solving business and daily life challenges.

- People rarely use right-brain skills such as creativity and pattern recognition.

- The majority of people are uninspired.

- People are most excited about social responsibility projects which support young people or children.

Based on these insights, the team created a social platform called bang. Art Innovation Prix that would support the productions of young artists and students from different disciplines including fine arts, engineering, design, and science. These works would be inspired by developments in bang (bites, atoms, neurons, genes) and powered by advanced technologies such as artificial intelligence, robotics, and biotech.

bang.Prix was designed as a platform where businesspeople support young people, and young people use projects incorporating non-linear thinking to inspire businesspeople . Project applications selected by the jury are supported by a mentor team including prominent people from academia, art, business, and technology.

In its first year, the platform supported and exhibited 14 artful and innovative ideas. The artworks inspired visitors from many organizations including large enterprises and startups. Its aura reached many people thanks to a strong presence in art and business newspapers and magazines. bang.prix became a real "prix" after exhibitions at different galleries, universities, art fairs, innovation and design events, and conferences.

In the second year of bang. Art Innovation Prix, young artists were invited to international art and innovation organizations. Artists from different countries also began to submit their projects to bang.prix. To accelerate the momentum of this energy, the ArtBizTech team kicked off a design thinking project aimed to "enhance the global mobility of artists by connecting digital art organizations in different countries." More than 100 digital artists, curators, and art directors from 20 different countries participated in the research phase. One outcome of the project was a "Global Digital Art Insight Report" designed to serve as a collection of ideas fostering non-linear thinking. The ArtBizTech team works with the motivation that bang. Art Innovation Prix not only helps young artists reach more art lovers all around the world but also helps them meet businesspeople who are in search of new sources of inspiration.

www.ingramcontent.com/pod-product-compliance
Lightning Source LLC
Chambersburg PA
CBHW081657270326
41933CB00017B/3195